"Nourish makes what otherwise seems like a daunting dietary change effortless and incredibly tasty. With this book as your guide, you will have endless ideas of dishes to prepare that will excite your palate as well as heal your body."

—MICKEY TRESCOTT, NTP, author of *The Autoimmune Paleo Cookbook*

"Rachael has created the ultimate cookbook for anyone on a restricted diet who just wants to enjoy food again. *Nourish* is packed with approachable recipes that build a foundation for eating healthily, feeding your body, and warming your soul. Rachael has masterfully developed big flavors and created internationally inspired dishes you've had to give up...until now. You can trust the recipes in *Nourish* to help you on your healing journey."

—STEPHANIE GAUDREAU, author of *The Performance Paleo Cookbook* and creator of Stupid Easy Paleo

"As someone who is struggling to make a lasting transition to an AIP-oriented diet, I want to share with all of you that Rachael's food is absolutely fantastic. Not only did I find myself in awe of how approachable her recipes are to prepare, but the ingredients are fully accessible for "normal" people in "normal" stores. My kids cleaned their plates every single time I served a recipe."

—CIARRA HANNAH, creator of Popular Paleo and author of *The Frugal Paleo Cookbook*

"Rachael gives you recipes that combine vegetables, fruits and meats in a way you may not have ever thought was possible. This cookbook has an amazing group of nutrient-dense recipes that not only taste fantastic, but will help your body heal. *Nourish* shows us that you don't have to sacrifice flavor in order to live a healthy lifestyle, and that following an autoimmune-friendly diet can be more delicious than you ever thought it could be!"

—AMY DENSMORE, founder of PaleoCupboard.Com

NOURISH

THE PALEO HEALING COOKBOOK

EASY YET FLAVORFUL RECIPES
THAT FIGHT AUTOIMMUNE ILLNESSES
FROM CELIAC DISEASE AND ARTHRITIS, TO MULTIPLE SCLEROSIS AND MORE

RACHAEL BRYANT
FOUNDER OF MEATIFIED

PAGE STREET
PUBLISHING CO.

PAGE STREET
PUBLISHING CO.

Copyright © 2015 Rachael Bryant

First published in 2015 by
Page Street Publishing Co.
27 Congress Street, Suite 103
Salem, MA 01970
www.pagestreetpublishing.com

Distributed by Macmillan; sales in Canada by The Canadian Manda Group; distribution in Canada by The Jaguar Book Group.

18   17   16   15   1   2   3   4   5

ISBN-13: 978-1-62414-102-7
ISBN-10: 1-62414-102-1

Library of Congress Control Number: 2014955231

Cover and book design by Page Street Publishing Co.
Photography by Rachael Bryant

Printed and bound in the USA

Page Street is proud to be a member of 1% for the Planet. Members donate one percent of their sales to one or more of the over 1,500 environmental and sustainability charities across the globe who participate in this program.

DEDICATION

To Mr. Meatified, who still doesn't know
what's in his fridge after
all these years.

CONTENTS

FOREWORD

Autoimmune disease has reached epidemic proportions with an estimated 50 million Americans afflicted. But, this doesn't have to be the case. As scientific research reveals more and more details of how food directly impacts the immune system, we are reaching a new understanding of the role that diet plays in autoimmune disease. This understanding includes identifying certain foods, many marketed as being "healthy" choices, as contributors to the rise of autoimmune disease. But of more importance, we are also able to distinguish a long list of health-promoting foods, foods that are rich in nutrients and devoid of inflammatory compounds, foods that thus can support immune system regulation and provide the body with the opportunity to heal.

The therapeutic value of food cannot be overemphasized. Vitamins, minerals, phytochemicals, essential amino acids, and essential fatty acids provide the raw materials for every chemical reaction and every cellular structure in the body. By consuming a variety of nutrient-dense foods, the body has the wealth of resources it needs to recover health. Furthermore, by avoiding those foods that can contribute to immune system dysfunction and by addressing lifestyle factors equally as important for immune system regulation, we can finally put an end to the brutal attacks of the immune system on our own tissues. We can put autoimmune disease into remission.

How to eat to restore normal immune system function and manage autoimmune disease has been formulated into a therapeutic diet called the Paleo diet autoimmune protocol (AIP), or the Paleo Approach. It is a diet that reflects everything we currently know about how food impacts health for the most sensitive among us, those of us with autoimmune disease. While it is a very powerful tool for regaining health, that doesn't mean that following this diet is easy. In fact, the autoimmune protocol can be overwhelming and just plain ol' difficult.

The biggest challenge to successfully following the autoimmune protocol is figuring out what to eat, and how to cook a more limited collection of ingredients into delicious and satisfying meals. Once mastered, you'll quickly see that food does still get to taste amazing and that you needn't feel deprived. However, it can feel like a pretty steep learning curve to get there. And that's where *Nourish* comes in.

Nourish is a masterful collection of innovative yet accessible recipes, which follow the strictest form of the autoimmune protocol, designed to get you eating this healing diet without even a second of missing out on flavor! With a focus on simple ingredients and straightforward cooking techniques, the range of scrumptious options will have you feeling pampered if not spoiled for choice. Can you think of anything better than improving your health with food so delicious you'll be closing your eyes while you eat to better savor every bite?

Better yet, *Nourish* gives you recipes that will have the whole family supporting you on your journey toward health. While you follow a therapeutic diet, everyone else at your table won't even notice that they're eating the healthiest foods available. With complex, bold and enticing flavors, *Nourish* delivers a meal that everyone will love. With *Nourish*, you get to do just that: nourish both your body and soul with the same amazing bite!

—Sarah Ballantyne, PhD, *New York Times* bestselling author of *The Paleo Approach* and *The Paleo Approach Cookbook*

Sarah Ballantyne

ABOUT THIS BOOK

When I first came across the Paleo autoimmune protocol, or AIP, I had two completely different, contradictory reactions. My first reaction as someone who was looking for relief from my Hashimoto's disease symptoms was totally optimistic and hopeful. I was excited: "Maybe *this* is the way I need to eat feel better!" My other reaction, even as someone who was already eating Paleo, was actually probably better described as a meltdown: "Well, what on earth *can* I eat, if I give up even *more* foods?"

Those two conflicting reactions were what prompted me to write this book. I want to make starting the AIP easy for *you*. If you're reading this, then I want you to know that it's absolutely possible to follow the AIP without feeling deprived, like you're on a diet or like there's nothing left in the kitchen to work with when it comes to making tasty meals. Every recipe in this book is 100 percent AIP-friendly, which takes the guesswork out of the elimination phase and makes it as smooth a transition as possible for you.

Now let's focus on my favorite thing: *flavor*! When you start off with what appears to be such a long list of AIP no's and not a lot of "yes, please" foods, it feels like you're going to be stuck eating boring, bland food. I really want to show you that doesn't have to be the case! It's possible to make boldly seasoned dishes with layers of flavor and still adhere to the AIP, I promise. The recipes in this book will show you how, with interesting food pairings and twists on classic dishes. I've tried to give you back the foods I never thought would be possible on the AIP. Got a craving for curry? I've got you covered. Missing internationally inspired dishes? You can have those. Want to make some comfort food? You still can!

For you moms and dads out there, never fear! You can bring these delicious, nutrient-dense foods straight into your regular meal rotation, without protest from the kids who will be happily eating this way right along with you. Because everybody loves delicious food! Familiar and easy-to-find ingredients form the base of these recipes, making it almost effortless to serve meals that have people asking for seconds.

The key to eating AIP is making the most of your kitchen time, without having to spend hours at the stove. I make this easy and approachable with simple cooking methods, make-ahead meals and batch cooking tips.

I hope you and your family love these recipes as much as we do!

INTRODUCTION

It is estimated that more than 50 million people have autoimmune diseases in America *alone*. Although the systems affected and symptoms present will vary from condition to condition and person to person, the underlying cause for at least 100 different diseases is an immune system that doesn't function as it should. Instead of protecting us from outside invaders like bacteria, parasites or viruses, the immune systems of those of us with autoimmune disease mistake our own cells and tissues for the very invaders from which they are supposed to protect us. A healthy person will create antibodies in response to an external threat, like, say, a virus, that then seek out, bind to and mark the virus as something that needs to be destroyed and removed from the body. However, people with autoimmune diseases actually create autoantibodies that attack healthy cells and tissues. Our bodies essentially turn on themselves (more on that later) and the cumulative damage that causes over time eventually manifests as symptoms of autoimmune disease, whether that's arthritis, which attacks the joints, or celiac disease, which attacks the small intestine, or Hashimoto's disease, which attacks the thyroid, just to name a few. Doesn't sound like much fun, does it?

When most people think about autoimmune disease, they think of it as something that is genetic; something that they cannot influence or treat proactively, other than by managing symptoms. That's certainly what I was told and believed when I was diagnosed years ago with Hashimoto's disease. I dutifully took my thyroid medication and thought that was all I could do, even though I continued to have symptoms and feel all-around terrible. But now for the good news: that's not necessarily true! While genetics are a necessary component in the development of autoimmune disease and can cause an individual to be genetically predisposed to producing the autoantibodies that lay the foundation for autoimmune disease, there are other contributing factors. Those necessary contributing factors are an individual's environment and their lifestyle, which includes diet.

Environmental factors trigger autoimmune disease and can include a range of different circumstances: illness and infection, exposure to chemicals, levels of stress and hormonal imbalances, among others. Lifestyle factors such as sleep, exercise and diet also play a role in triggering autoimmune diseases and flares. But now for some more good news: those environmental and lifestyle factors can be managed or even removed! What does that mean? That it is possible to get rid of those autoimmune disease triggers, stop autoimmune flares and symptoms and begin to heal from the inside out. Ultimately, it's possible to encourage your body to stop attacking itself, repair the damage it has done and even get healthy again!

But before I can tell you a bit more about the "how" of all of this, I need to tell you a little bit more about the "why" of autoimmune disease. There's a common thread that ties all autoimmune diseases together, regardless of the symptoms, systems affected or specific disease. It's kind of a mouthful, so brace yourself: increased intestinal permeability. Lucky for you, I'm just going to go ahead and refer to that from now on as "leaky gut." Research into autoimmune disease seems to show that it is a necessary precursor to the development of autoimmune disease.

WHAT'S LEAKY GUT?

"Leaky gut" means that the intestines have become more permeable than they should be. The gut is a barrier that is supposed to take in the things the body needs (like nutrients from food) and prevent things that should be exiting the body (like bacteria or food waste) from getting into the body. When the intestinal barrier becomes more permeable, it begins to allow things into the body that shouldn't be present. That, in turn, triggers the immune response needed for autoimmune disease to develop. I talked a little earlier about how environment and lifestyle are contributing factors in the development of autoimmune disease: that is because leaky gut is caused by environment and lifestyle. What does that mean? That leaky gut can be healed through changing those environmental and lifestyle factors, including diet. So if leaky gut is necessary for the development of autoimmune disease, but it is caused by diet and lifestyle factors, here's the important take away: it is possible to heal a leaky gut by addressing those factors. In doing so, you can begin to heal from your autoimmune disease!

SO HOW DO I BEGIN TO HEAL?

When I first started on my healing journey, I began by adopting the Paleo diet. That meant removing all grains, beans, legumes, processed oils, dairy products and refined sugar from my diet. I originally turned to eating Paleo as a way of dealing with my own Hashimoto's symptoms. I found that it dramatically improved and reduced the weird nagging side effects that still persisted, even though my blood tests were all coming back "normal." The thing was, though, that I still didn't feel normal. Some of the symptoms had gone, but quite a few were still hanging on determinedly!

And that's when I learned about the Paleo autoimmune protocol, or AIP, through the work of Dr. Sarah Ballantyne, PhD, also known through her website as the Paleo Mom. Sarah studied the science behind autoimmunity and came up with the dietary modifications necessary to adapt the Paleo diet for people with autoimmune diseases. Sarah clearly laid out the definitive guide to the AIP in her book *The Paleo Approach,* and all of the recipes in this book comply with the protocol that she devised.

All of the foods and substances that are disallowed on the AIP are those that contribute to causing leaky gut by causing irritation and damage to the gut. They are also foods that are nutrient deficient and hormonal disruptors. Removing them means that the gut is not being constantly irritated or damaged and our hormones aren't being constantly disrupted. In turn, this provides the environment in which the gut can begin to heal and autoimmune disease symptoms can begin to lessen and even improve. Which is what we all want, right?

The AIP starts with an elimination period of at least 60 days in which these damaging and nutrient-deficient foods are removed completely from the diet to give the gut a chance to heal. Cutting out these foods also promotes hormonal regulation, which, in turn, facilitates further healing of the immune system. Sounds neat, huh? So here's the list of foods to be avoided on the AIP:

- grains
- dairy products
- legumes
- processed vegetable oils and sugars
- eggs

- nuts and seeds
- nightshades
- coffee
- alcohol

While fruit is allowed on the AIP, the aim is to keep fructose levels lower than 20 grams per day since excessive fructose can also be problematic while healing the gut.

WHAT THE HECK ARE NIGHTSHADES?

So I told you we're not supposed to eat nightshades on the AIP. But what *is* a nightshade? Ever heard of belladonna...also known as deadly nightshade? It's as poisonous as it sounds and is one plant in a botanical family with thousands of varieties, including other not-so-friendly plants like tobacco. While most of us don't tend to think about nightshades in our day-to-day life, when it comes to the AIP, we do need to know about the edible plants from the nightshade family so we can avoid them.

The nightshade family as a whole contains substances that are irritating to and can damage the gut, and provoke an autoimmune response—which is exactly what we are trying to avoid by following the AIP! Here is a list of the most common edible nightshade plants that are avoided while on the AIP:

- bell peppers and "sweet" peppers
- chili peppers of all types
- eggplant

- pimentos
- potatoes (not including sweet potatoes)
- tomatoes and tomatillos

And while we are avoiding nightshades, we want to also avoid the spices and seasonings that are derived from nightshade plants, such as:

- cayenne pepper
- chili pepper flakes
- chili powder

- curry powder
- paprika
- red pepper flakes

WHAT ABOUT OTHER SPICES?

As I mentioned earlier, since we're cutting out all not-tummy-friendly seeds as part of the AIP, we also need to know about other spices and seasonings that are derived from seeds so that we can avoid them, too. Here's a quick list:

- celery seed
- coriander seed (the leaves, cilantro, are fine)
- cumin
- dill seed (the leaves are fine)
- fennel seed (the plant's bulb is fine)

- fenugreek seed
- mustard
- poppy seeds
- sesame seeds

Trying to avoid these nightshade and seed-based spices also means being exceptionally careful when it comes to buying or using prepared spice blends. Read the labels carefully, or make your own. Don't worry—every recipe in this book is 100 percent safe for the elimination phase and cuts out the guesswork for you!

SO WHAT *CAN* YOU EAT?

It's at about this time after reeling over that list of "can't have" foods that people start to look at me as if I've sprouted 17 new heads. I know, it sounds like a challenge. It's at times like these that I feel like the Severus Snape of the food world: I'm the killjoy with a bunch of mean rules that are designed to make you suffer... but all the while, I've actually been working on a plan for your own good. Really. I promise. Pinky swear.

Even people who have been eating Paleo for quite some time can balk at the idea of giving up eggs for breakfast, their coffee habit and their nut-flour-based treats. Like I mentioned earlier, I did myself! But the AIP isn't about restriction. This book is going to show you that even eating a "restrictive" AIP-compliant diet can be simple, delicious and varied. You just need to know where to start. So here's a list of foods that *are* allowed while following the Paleo autoimmune protocol and are the building blocks for tasty meals:

- all meats, including offal and bone broths

- healthy fats, such as avocado, olive oil and animal fats (yes, really!)

- all vegetables (except nightshades)

- all fruits (except nightshades)

- all herbs and seasonings that come from the leaves of plants

- some spices

- lacto-fermented, probiotic foods and drinks, such as sauerkraut and other vegetables, kombucha and water kefir

- coconut products such as coconut oil, milk and cream (coconut flour and coconut flakes are okay, but only in moderation)

That list may not look like much, but my recipes are here to help! Did you know that it's possible to enjoy a curry dish without tomatoes or dairy products? Or that you can make tailgate-worthy wings without hot sauce? How about a grain-free alternative to croutons? Well, you can—and I've created the recipes in this cookbook to show you how!

ARE NON-AIP FOODS GONE FOREVER?

Remember when I talked about healing the gut earlier? That's the beauty of the AIP. It does start with an elimination period where lots of familiar foods are gone. But once that elimination period is up, there is a reintroduction process through which you can figure out which of those foods on the no-fly lists above you may be able to tolerate.

It's a personalized process: Over time, as the gut heals by following AIP principles throughout the elimination period and as you begin reintroducing foods slowly afterwards, you can figure out the foods that trigger autoimmune disease flares for you personally and those that you can safely eat once you have healed, even though they're not technically part of the AIP template. You might find that you are able to reintroduce eggs successfully, but no longer tolerate coffee. Conversely, somebody else might not be able to deal with eggs, but will find that they are A-OK with seed spices.

The even better news? As you continue to adapt AIP for you, your gut will continue to heal. Which means that you will have a chance to try reintroducing foods again at a later time if you so choose.

In the meantime, though, all the recipes in this book have been tailored to fit within the AIP elimination period. I'm going to take out all of the guesswork for you and show you how to eat delicious food that nourishes your body and heals you from the inside out. Yay!

IT'S NOT JUST ABOUT REMOVING THINGS...

Taking away the foods that damage the gut and promote inflammatory responses is obviously a huge part of beginning to heal from autoimmune disease. But it's just as important to start *adding* things to your lifestyle. There are things other than food to consider: Making sure you get regular exercise, plenty of good quality sleep, minimizing stress and even getting outside in the sun are all important things to work on while healing.

But I'm here to talk about the food—my favorite thing!—and show you how AIP-friendly food can be fabulous. Not only can it taste great, but it can nourish you in a way that is going to help you heal. Can you guess what the best foods are to help you heal? They are all nutrient-dense foods.

NUTRIENT DENSITY

Earlier I listed the foods that we *don't* want to eat while following the AIP, since one of the key elements of healing is avoiding the things that are not beneficial to the gut, such as alcohol, grains, legumes and sugars, while also removing the foods that are most likely to provoke an unhealthy immune response (and are potentially allergenic), such as eggs, soy, nuts, nightshades, seeds and dairy products. What I want to focus on now, though, is what is left to work with: a *huge* variety of meats, seafood, fruits, vegetables and healthy fats, as well as herbs and seasonings. All of these ingredients will provide you with the nutrition you need to help regulate your immune system and heal—all while eating delicious and satisfying food.

The key to successfully following the AIP for healing revolves around the idea of nutrient density. In order to heal, we want to eat foods that are as nutrient dense as possible. In fact, it's important to note that autoimmune diseases are actually linked to poor diets that are lacking vitamins, minerals and other essential nutrients. The AIP is based on the idea of eating nutrient-dense foods—those that are as health-promoting and as nutritious as possible. Foods that contain the valuable vitamins and minerals we need, as well as antioxidants, essential amino acids and fatty acids like omega-3s. These are the foods that will help us get rid of inflammation, regulate our immune systems and become the building blocks of better health. Eating a nutrient dense diet that has plenty of meat, seafood, vegetables and quality fats is the best way to bring about optimal health and healing!

When we talk about nutrient density, we also mean trying to eat as much variety as possible. Sure, eating beef and kale every day would technically be AIP compliant, but it wouldn't give you the variety of different nutrients you need—not to mention the fact that it would be incredibly boring! Eating a nutrient-dense diet also means mixing things up a little! Try to get as many different foods as possible into your day—that way, you're getting an array of different nutritional benefits.

Nutrient density is also important for another reason. Taste! Who wants to eat the same meals week in and week out? Nobody! Following the AIP doesn't have to be dull—and learning to make a variety of different meals from diverse ingredients can be as fun as it is delicious. The recipes in this book are designed to help you make food that embraces these health-enhancing principles, while showing you that you have so many more options than you realized!

MEAT MATTERS

When it comes to food and maximizing the healing process, it's important to emphasize that quality matters. An important component of the AIP is incorporating good-quality, grass-fed or pasture-raised meats wherever possible within your budget. Why the focus on these kinds of meats? They are much more nutrient dense than meat from conventionally farmed animals. Grass-fed and pasture-raised meat is higher in essential vitamins and minerals, and has a healthier, lower ratio of omega-6 to omega-3 fatty acids. The meat from grass-fed animals is leaner than that from conventionally farmed animals because they get so much more exercise, yet that fat is also healthier because it has greater levels of vitamin D from the time they spend outdoors.

Of course, there's a catch: this higher-quality meat can be more expensive than conventionally farmed meat. But there are ways to make good-quality meat fit into your budget and this cookbook has plenty of recipes that will help you do so. Ground meat is one of the best ways to incorporate grass-fed meat into your meals and I've included meals that help you reinvigorate and reinvent this staple in tasty, healing recipes. I'll show you how to make gut-healing, inexpensive broths and how to incorporate them into meals without even realizing it. Cheaper cuts can be transformed with a little imagination and mastering some simple cooking methods, which is why you'll find plenty of slow cooker and "low and slow" oven recipes in this book. In fact, those slow-cooking methods are some of the best ways to get all the nutrition from the meat you're cooking, breaking down the meat so that you can get the benefits of collagen and amino acids from the connective tissues and bones. I'll even show you how to incorporate organ meats into your diet in ways that are truly delicious, because they are the most nutrient-dense (and cheap!) protein options out there.

SOLD ON SEAFOOD

As important as it is to include good-quality meats in our diets, it's probably even more important to include seafood in our meals regularly, because its nutrition profile is the perfect balance to the kinds of meat we were talking about earlier. If you want to get a boost of vitamins A and D and minerals like selenium, then you need to be looking seaward to get your fix!

Certain types of seafood are also amazing sources of healthy omega-3 fatty acids. We definitely want those in our diet for their fantastic anti-inflammatory benefits, and this is even more important if you eat chicken or poultry regularly. Our feathered friends may be delicious, but they're high in the not-so-helpful omega-6 fatty acids and it's important to have a healthy balance of omega-3 to omega-6 fatty acids. Seafood really is a superfood—if you eat seafood several times a week, it can help balance out those fatty acid ratios.

When it comes to keeping the budget balanced, seafood is one of the most economical choices, too. Frozen wild-caught seafood is a great protein choice that can be much cheaper than red meat options, especially if you keep an eye out for sales. It's a great "convenience food," too—it's easy and quick to thaw fish fillets or a package of shrimp, which is often a savior for me when it comes to weeknight meals. The other easy option for meals or even a snack is good-quality, BPA-free canned seafood. Canned fish can be way more exciting than tuna: broaden your horizons to the wonders of oily fish like sardines and mackerel or even clams and smoked oysters! All of these little marine prizes can be made into snacks or even a meal in minutes!

PICK YOUR PRODUCE

Just as variety and quality are what we want when it comes to meat, the same is true of our produce. Buy the best possible fruits and vegetables you can find. If you can shop locally and seasonally, that's the absolute best way to broaden your horizons—and probably save a dollar or two! Don't stick to the same old favorites. Mix it up! Try something new, or try preparing vegetables you're not so crazy about in a different way. We want to eat as many different types of vegetables (and fruits) as possible, and we should be aiming for at least two different vegetables on every plate, to get the fullest possible range of healing nutrients.

To help you out, you'll find a huge range of ways to incorporate plenty of fresh produce into your meals throughout this cookbook, with some fun and inventive flavor pairings. Vegetables aren't just for soups, salads and sides—although this book has those, too. Most of the meals in this cookbook use plenty of produce! Without having dairy products and grain-based flours to turn to, I've gotten inventive when it comes to making sauces, creating the right texture in a dish or holding things like meatballs together. Which means that this book is full of recipes with "hidden" vegetables! Maybe don't tell the mini humans about that part...

FACT: IT'S ALL ABOUT THE FATS

Did you know that the immune system requires fats? In a world where we've all been indoctrinated into the idea that fat is bad and low-fat products are our saviors, it seems hard to believe that we NEED fats. But we do! Our immune systems need fatty acids to function—and I'm talking about both the much-maligned saturated fats as well as monounsaturated fats. Fats are actually essential to the absorption of the fat-soluble vitamins A, D and K—which can all help restore the gut barrier. Clearly, we need our (good) fats!

But here's the kicker, not all fats are created equal. You'll notice that most of the recipes in this book call for coconut or avocado oil as the main cooking fats. The fact is, in most cases, you could easily substitute whatever AIP-friendly fat you like for those recommendations. The reason I listed those two is because they're the most common, easy-to-find AIP-friendly fats, they're pretty neutral-tasting, and they're usually liquid at room temperature (although coconut oil will solidify when it's cooler), which makes them easy to pour or measure. They also have higher smoke points than some of the other options, which makes them suitable for frying. With that said, like with meat and produce, eating a variety of fats is a good thing. Some other options include:

- bacon fat from pasture-raised pigs

- virgin or extra-virgin olive oil (for salads or finishing, not cooking)

- lard rendered from pasture-raised pigs

- palm oil or shortening (make sure it is sustainably sourced)

- tallow rendered from grass-fed beef or lamb

If you have access to these fats or have time to render them yourself, feel free to use them whenever and wherever you like!

WHAT TO REMEMBER

So here's the summary. Following the AIP means basing your daily meals on meat, seafood, vegetables, fats and a little fruit, while eating as many different varieties of those foods as possible to maximize nutrient density. So get this: There's no fad, there's no gimmick and there's no messing around. Eating good-quality, real food while avoiding the things that can trigger immune responses is the key to regulating your immune system and healing from the inside out! Isn't that pretty freaking amazing?

BRING ON BREAKFAST!

So often, traditional breakfast foods are either grain or egg-centric, so when those things are removed from our plates, it can be tough to imagine what on earth is left to eat. Personally, I don't like to look at it that way—there are still so many delicious, amazing foods out there while following the AIP. So here's my take: You know how people love "breakfast for dinner"? I love to have dinner for breakfast! Seriously, there's no reason that you can't enjoy a nourishing bowl of soup first thing in the morning. Or delicious leftover roast chicken and vegetables. Or even a beautiful colorful salad in the summer. Look at it this way: Breakfast is just whatever you eat as your first meal of the day!

Having said that, I remember all too well how it wasn't easy to make that adjustment when I first started following the AIP. It can be difficult and overwhelming to give up familiar tastes and textures, especially when it comes to a meal that plenty of people aren't used to having to think about—it's easy to pour some cereal in a bowl, or maybe fry an egg. It's not so easy to come around to eating greens first thing—although I promise you that in time, you'll think nothing of it. So here I've given you a few starter recipes that will bridge the gap from familiar food territory to "anything goes" eating in the morning! Remember to mix things up: Have a side of protein with your Coconut "Oatmeal" (page 20) or a side of fruit along with your sausage and Plantain Hash Browns (page 28). Don't eat the same foods all the time—make sure you're getting a mix of protein, carbs and good fats for the best possible start to your day. These recipes are just the beginning when it comes to breakfast!

When you're feeling a little more adventurous, try out these recipes in the morning: Apple & Cucumber Salad with Smoked Salmon (page 162), Thai Chicken Soup (page 48) or Slow Cooker Bison "Chili" (page 43).

COCONUT "OATMEAL"
FIVE WAYS

This recipe is a little sneaky, because it's actually vegetable based! Surprisingly, it's the vegetable base that makes this recipe so similar to the texture of oatmeal: the squash gives a creamy texture and natural sweetness, while the coconut provides a great, slightly chewy texture. Unlike those creepy little packets of microwavable grains, this recipe is a great source of healthy carbs in the morning, without the junk! It's also super easy and endlessly adaptable—plus it can be made ahead. I like to make up a batch on the weekend, divide it into portions and stash it in the fridge, that way I have easy grab and go breakfast portions at hand. Pair your bowl of "oatmeal" with some protein on the side and you've got a simple, easy breakfast that won't weird out your coworkers!

MAKES 4–6 SERVINGS

1 acorn squash (about 2 cups [400 g] when cooked)

1¼ cups (300 ml) coconut milk

¾ cup (60 g) unsweetened shredded coconut

1 tbsp (15 ml) honey

1 tsp (1 g) ground cinnamon

Pinch of salt

ROAST: Preheat the oven to 400°F (205°C). Cut the acorn squash in half lengthwise. Pour enough water into a baking dish to cover the bottom and then add the acorn squash halves to the dish, cut-side facing down. Roast the acorn squash until just tender, about 40 minutes. Remove from the oven and place the acorn squash halves onto a plate. Allow to cool slightly before scraping out and discarding the seeds.

COOK: Scoop out the acorn squash halves and add the flesh to a small saucepan over low-medium heat. Add all the remaining ingredients to the pan and stir gently to combine. Bring the "oatmeal" to a simmer and cook until heated through and thickened. Serve warm with your favorite fresh fruit toppings.

VARIATIONS: This Coconut "Oatmeal" can form the base of almost endless flavor combinations. Just add the following ingredients to the basic recipe above and heat until warm. Here are some of my favorites!

APPLE CINNAMON

1 apple, peeled, cored and chopped

1 cup (240 ml) unsweetened applesauce

1 tsp (1 g) ground cinnamon

PUMPKIN SPICE

1 cup (240 ml) pumpkin puree

1 tbsp (15 ml) maple syrup

1 tsp (1 g) ground cinnamon

¼ tsp ground mace

CHERRY "CHOCOLATE"

1 cup (120 g) cherries, pitted and chopped

2 tbsp (30 ml) honey

2 tsp (4 g) carob powder

BERRIES & CREAM

1 cup (230 g) frozen mixed berries

¼ cup (60 ml) coconut cream

1 tbsp (15 ml) maple syrup

Pulse the frozen mixed berries in a mini food processor before stirring them into the pan. This step is optional but helps to distribute the berry flavor more evenly through the "oatmeal"—plus it gives a fun speckled look that kids will love!

SLOW COOKER BREAKFAST MEATLOAF
WITH CHERRY SAUCE

One of the easiest things to rely on for breakfast in the morning is homemade sausage patties. But it's time-consuming to shape them individually and cook them in the morning. This meatloaf has all the flavor of a breakfast sausage, with the sliceable texture of meatloaf and is great to have ready-to-go in the morning. Here's what I do: Make the meatloaf in the evening, then refrigerate it overnight. When we're ready for breakfast, all I need to do is slice off what I need and then gently reheat it in a skillet for a few minutes. Gelatin is great for gut health, but here it's working overtime as a replacement binder instead of eggs to make it AIP friendly. And if you're really in a rush, this meatloaf is delicious cold, too!

MAKES 8 – 10 SLICES

1 tbsp (15 ml) coconut or avocado oil

2 cups (280 g) diced onion

½ cup (120 ml) Chicken Broth (page 225)

2 tsp (5 g) powdered gelatin

2 tsp (8 g) garlic powder

2 tsp (2 g) dried oregano leaves

2 tsp (1 g) ground sage

2 tsp (2 g) dried thyme leaves

1 tsp (5 g) salt

1½ cups (90 g) crushed pork rinds

2 lbs (900 g) lean ground pork

Cherry Sauce (page 214)

SOFTEN: Heat the oil in a small skillet and cook the onions until they are just softened, about 5 minutes. Remove the onions from the heat and set aside to cool. Add the chicken broth to a bowl. Sprinkle the gelatin powder over the broth to bloom, which will take a few minutes.

MIX: In a large bowl, mix together the garlic powder, oregano, sage, thyme, salt and the crushed pork rinds with the cooked and cooled onion. Add the ground pork and the bloomed gelatin to the bowl: Use your hands to mix the meatloaf until all the ingredients are evenly combined and the mixture holds together.

SHAPE: Transfer the meatloaf mixture to the insert of a large, 6-quart (5.5 L) slow cooker. Press the meatloaf mixture together and shape it so that it matches the shape of the insert, taking care to leave enough space around the meatloaf so that it does not touch the sides. Smooth the top of the meatloaf and then cook on low until the internal temperature is 150°F (66°C)—about 2 hours and 45 minutes. Once the meatloaf is cooked, remove the slow cooker insert and place it on a cooling rack, uncovered, for about 30 minutes. This will make it easier to remove the meatloaf without it breaking.

SAUCE: While the meatloaf is cooling, make the Cherry Sauce and keep warm until ready to serve. Once the meatloaf has cooled, use two large spatulas to slide under the meatloaf and remove it from the slow cooker insert, placing it on a cutting board. Slice the meatloaf and serve each slice topped with a little of the Cherry Sauce.

KEDGEREE
WITH SMOKED HADDOCK

I know, right? What the heck is kedgeree? The original version of the dish is a mishmash of curried rice and smoked fish, often topped with hard-boiled eggs. Believe it or not, it was a breakfast dish! Nutritionally, though, that makes sense: this dish has plenty of healthy fats from the smoked haddock, as well as carbs from the "rice," which makes it perfect for keeping you full until lunchtime. Here I've ditched the eggs, swapped out the rice for shredded white sweet potato and replaced the nightshade-filled commercial curry powder for a combination of anti-inflammatory and warming spices. I used to hate kedgeree as a kid; now I find myself craving it as comfort food.

SERVES 4

---

2 lbs (900 g) white sweet potato (about 2 large)

2 tbsp (30 ml) coconut or avocado oil

1 cup (140 g) onion, diced

2½ tbsp (4 g) dried fenugreek leaves

1 tbsp (6 g) ground ginger

1 tsp (1 g) ground cinnamon

1 tsp (5 g) salt

1 tsp (2 g) ground turmeric

½ tsp ground mace

13 oz (365 g) smoked haddock or kippers

½ cup (120 ml) coconut milk

¼ cup (10 g) fresh flat-leaf parsley, chopped

SOFTEN: Peel the sweet potatoes and grate them coarsely, using either a box grater or the grater attachment on your food processor. Lay out the shredded sweet potato on a clean dish towel. Wrap the towel around the sweet potato and squeeze gently to remove any excess moisture. Leave the shredded sweet potato wrapped in the towel while you heat the oil in a large skillet. Add the diced onion to the hot oil and cook until softened but not beginning to brown, about 5 minutes. Add the shredded sweet potato to the pan and stir to evenly coat with oil.

SEASON: Add the fenugreek, ginger, cinnamon, salt, turmeric and mace to the pan. Stir so that the spices are evenly distributed. Cook until the sweet potato begins to soften and is almost but not quite cooked through, about 5 minutes. Drain and discard any oil or brine from the smoked haddock or kippers, then flake the fish into the pan. Stir in the coconut milk and cook until the fish is warmed through and the coconut milk is absorbed. The sweet potato should be cooked through, but not soft—it should still have a little bite, similar to *al dente* pasta or rice. Sprinkle with the fresh chopped parsley and serve immediately!

NOT CRAZY ABOUT COCONUT? You can easily omit the coconut milk from the recipe.

SAUSAGE GRAVY "BENEDICT"
IN PORTOBELLO MUSHROOM CAPS

This is a play on two of my former favorite breakfast recipes—eggs benedict and sausage gravy. Gone is the bread—instead, I've topped spinach with roasted portobello mushrooms and ladled over a rich creamy-but-cream-less sausage gravy. The result is savory, comforting and somewhat addictive—and what's not to love about being able to turn hidden vegetables and broth into gravy? I often make the gravy up in advance. If I don't want to deal with an extra step in the morning, I simply add more broth to make a soup version of the gravy and add greens, then refrigerate the soup in single portions that I can grab first thing to reheat. Easy!

SERVES 4

1 tbsp (15 ml) coconut or avocado oil

1 cup (140 g) onion, diced

2 cloves garlic, minced

⅔ lb (300 g) cauliflower florets

2 cups (480 ml) Pork or Chicken Broth (page 225), divided

1 bay leaf

1 lb (454 g) Italian sausage (see Note)

1 tsp (1 g) dried oregano leaves

¾ tsp garlic powder

½ tsp dried thyme leaves

¼ tsp dried rosemary leaves

¼ tsp ground sage

Salt, to taste

4 portobello mushrooms

12 oz (340 g) fresh spinach

PREP: Add the oil to a saucepan over low heat and cook the onion and garlic until softened, about 5 minutes. Break the cauliflower florets into bite size pieces and add to the sauce pan, along with 1 cup (240 ml) of the pork or chicken broth and the bay leaf. Cover the pan with a lid and raise the heat to bring the broth to a gentle simmer. Cook until the cauliflower is just tender, about 10–15 minutes. While the vegetables are cooking, remove the sausage from its casings and cook over medium heat in a skillet, using the back of a spoon or spatula to break it up into smaller pieces. Cook the sausage until it is nicely browned, then remove the skillet from the heat and transfer the cooked sausage to a plate with a slotted spoon, reserving any excess fat in the skillet to cook the spinach in later.

BLEND: Remove the bay leaf from the sauce pan and transfer the cooked vegetables to a blender. Add the remaining pork or chicken broth and blend until smooth, then add ½ cup (70 g) of the cooked Italian sausage. Blend again until you have a smooth gravy. Transfer the gravy back into the saucepan and stir through the remaining cooked sausage. Taste the gravy at this point, then season with the oregano, garlic, thyme, rosemary and sage, if needed (see Note below). Add salt, to taste, and keep the gravy warm on the stovetop.

ROAST: Preheat the oven to 400°F (205°C). Line a baking tray with parchment paper. Wipe the mushrooms clean with a damp paper towel to remove any dirt. Remove the stems and scrape out most of the gills, leaving them intact along the edge—this will stop the mushroom caps from flattening when they are roasted. Roast the mushrooms for 15 minutes, until just tender. While the mushrooms are roasting, wilt the spinach. Heat the skillet with the reserved sausage fat over medium heat and add the spinach a few handfuls at a time, cooking until just wilted. Remove the roasted mushrooms from the oven and pat the inside of the caps dry so that the mushroom juices do not water down the gravy. Divide the spinach between four plates, then top each with a mushroom cap. Spoon the warmed sausage gravy into the mushrooms and serve immediately!

NOTE: Make sure that the Italian sausage doesn't contain any seed or nightshade spices. If you can't find any AIP-friendly sausage, you can always make your own! Use a not-so-lean cut of pork as your ground-pork base and add your own seasoning. Check out the seasoning used in the Slow Cooker Breakfast Meatloaf (page 23) for inspiration.

PLANTAIN HASH BROWNS
WITH SUPER CRISPY EDGES

I think we can all agree that the crispy bits on traditional hash browns are the best part. Those soggy middles? Not so much. Using shredded plantain instead of white potatoes not only puts AIP-friendly hash browns back on the menu, but it seriously maximizes all those delicious crispy bits, as plantains just love being fried and are starchy enough to hold together on their own. Just like regular potato hash browns, these guys can be paired with both savory and sweet toppings because they're a mild-flavored starch. That means that these hash browns are just as good topped with breakfast sausage as they are with berries, maple syrup and whipped coconut cream.

MAKES 6

1½ cups (200 g) peeled and shredded green plantain (about 2)

1 tsp (5 g) salt, plus extra to taste

Coconut or avocado oil for frying

SOAK: Put the shredded plantain in a bowl and add enough water to cover, along with 1 teaspoon of salt. Let the shredded plantain soak for 5 minutes. Discard the saltwater and gently press any excess liquid from the plantain. Lay the shredded plantain on a cloth or paper towel and squeeze out any remaining liquid.

FRY: Divide the shredded plantain into 6 even portions, using a ¼-cup (60-ml) measuring cup. Use a little extra oil on your hands to stop the plantain sticking when you form the portions into patties. Pour enough oil into the skillet that at least half of the shredded plantain patties will be covered. Heat the oil over medium-high: the oil needs to be hot enough that the shredded plantain will sizzle when added, but not splatter. Working in batches as needed, cook the hash browns until golden-brown, about a minute per side. Pop the cooked hash browns onto a paper towel–lined plate to absorb any extra oil before serving.

BUTTERNUT SQUASH SKILLET
WITH LEEKS AND SPINACH

This skillet hash can do double duty as a side dish or a breakfast base. I love to make this in the morning and throw in whatever leftover cooked protein I have on hand: it works with everything from chopped chicken to sausage crumbles or bacon. The sweetness of the butternut pairs perfectly with the slight bitterness of the spinach and the warm flavor of the sage brings everything together. This is also a great way to get additional gut-healing collagen onto your plate in the morning because everything cooks in and absorbs that lovely chicken broth! I like to make this ahead of time and then simply reheat it in the morning.

SERVES 4

1 tbsp (15 ml) coconut or avocado oil

2 leeks, white and pale-green parts only, chopped into ¼-inch (6-mm) crescents

12 oz (340 g) peeled butternut squash, chopped into bite-size pieces

1 cup (240 ml) Chicken Broth (page 225)

1 tsp (4 g) garlic powder

1 tsp (2 g) ground sage

½ tsp salt

1 tbsp (15 ml) lemon juice

1 cup (120 g) thawed and drained frozen spinach, chopped

COOK: Add the oil to a hot skillet over medium heat and cook the chopped leeks until they begin to soften but not brown, about 5 minutes. Add the butternut squash, chicken broth, garlic, ground sage and salt, then cover and steam for 15 minutes, stirring occasionally to prevent sticking. Uncover the pan and cook for another 5 minutes, or until the liquid in the pan has almost all been absorbed. Add the lemon juice and the spinach to the pan and cook until the spinach is hot and the butternut squash is just fork tender, about another 5–10 minutes.

MAXIMIZING MEAT

The caveman cliché is hard to avoid when it comes to first exploring the Paleo way of eating. As a result, it's easy to envision that the AIP might be made up of meat-centric menus filled with giant servings of (expensive) steak at every meal. That causes a problem—it's easy to assume that the AIP must be extremely costly. The recipes in this chapter will show you that following the AIP doesn't have to break the bank—and that there's more to eating well than Fred Flintstone–size meals!

We've talked a little about how it's important to buy the best quality meat you can afford to get the best health benefits—this chapter will show you how to do that in a budget-friendly way! I'll show you how to season and flavor inexpensive ground-meat dishes that are nevertheless packed with international flavors, like Baked Swedish Meatballs (page 36) and Pastitsio Pie (page 61). You'll learn how to use cheaper and perhaps unfamiliar cuts of meat and transform them through simple long oven-braising or slow-cooker methods into mouthwatering meals like Slow Cooker Pork Shanks with Mushroom Gravy (page 88) or tender Perfect Sliced Roast Beef (page 59), the homemade alternative to commercially processed cold cuts. I'll even show you tasty ways to incorporate those nutritional powerhouses: organ meats. If you think you don't like liver, you need to try The Ultimate Liver Hater's Pâte (page 68)!

This chapter has a little something for everyone. I've tried to include quick weeknight meals like Beef & Broccoli Slaw Stir-Fry (page 97), along with one-pot meals like Braised Spring Chicken (page 79). I really wanted to show you that AIP-friendly food can be packed with flavor. It doesn't have to be bland or boring! Coming into the AIP, it seems at first like you'll never be able to enjoy some of your favorite foods again. But don't worry! Got a craving for curry? Try the Chicken Curry (page 83). How about a hankering for Thai food? Try the Grilled Thai Beef Skewers (page 49). This chapter shows how versatile the AIP can be...and how many food options are still there for you. So get cooking and tuck in!

CHICKEN STREET TACOS
WITH BLUEBERRY SALSA & AVOCADO CREAM

This is probably one of my favorite recipes of all time. Why? Well, it turns often-uninspiring leftover shredded chicken into an awesome AIP "taco" by piling it on top of thinly sliced jicama—no grain products needed. What's not to love about messy food that you *have* to eat with your hands?! My favorite part is the blueberry salsa: It's a little unexpected and adds a great not-too-sweet fruity flavor that is delicious alongside the avocado cream. Don't skip the cinnamon—it's what makes the salsa so darned addictive!

MAKES 12–16 MINI TACOS

FOR THE BLUEBERRY SALSA
1 cup (150 g) blueberries
¼ cup (35 g) onion, diced
2 tbsp (5 g) cilantro leaves, chopped
1 tbsp (15 ml) lime juice
Pinch of ground cinnamon

FOR THE AVOCADO CREAM
½ cup (120 g) mashed avocado
¼ cup + 2 tbsp (60 ml + 30 ml) coconut milk
2 tsp (10 ml) fresh lime juice
Pinch of salt
Handful of chopped fresh cilantro leaves to garnish

FOR THE CHICKEN "TACOS"
1 jicama
2 cups (200 g) leftover chicken, shredded

SQUISH: In a bowl, mix together all the blueberry salsa ingredients. Press down on the blueberries lightly with the back of a spoon to release some of their juices. Stir to combine and set aside for now.

BLEND: In a mini food processor or similar, add all the avocado cream ingredients. Process until smooth and creamy. Add a splash or two of water if it is too thick. Set aside while you make the "tacos."

ASSEMBLE: Peel the jicama and slice off the top and bottom. Use a mandoline set at approximately ⅛ inch (3 mm) and slice the jicama into 12–16 slices. The slices need to be thin enough to act as foldable "tacos," but not so thin that they crack easily. Divide the jicama slices between plates and use them as a base for your "tacos." Top the tacos with the shredded chicken, followed by the blueberry salsa and a scoop of avocado cream. You can pick these bad boys up and chow down on them just like the real thing!

NOT CRAZY ABOUT COCONUT? Leave out the coconut milk and add an extra ¼ cup (60 g) of mashed avocado and 1 teaspoon (5 ml) of lime juice. Alternatively, serve the tacos with the Grilled Pineapple Guacamole (page 213).

CHICKEN FRIED STEAK
WITH CREAMY ONION GRAVY

Anybody who has tried to make egg-free breading knows how sad that stuff can be. It can fall off completely if you try to fry it, or end up frustratingly soggy when you try to bake it. The usual go-to for Paleo peeps when it comes to trying to make a crispy coating is usually a nut flour—which is totally out of the question for us AIP-ers. The good news? I've spent hours in the kitchen testing different egg- and nut-free breading versions, so you don't have to! The trick to making it stick is a little strange: adding a little ground chicken blended into some coconut milk, which provides the necessary protein to make the breading layers bind. Trust me on this one, it works perfectly. This recipe has all the comfort-food qualities you're looking for: tender beef, a crispy coating and a rich, creamy gravy with just a hint of herbs.

SERVES 4-6 (DEPENDING ON THE SIZE OF YOUR CUBE STEAKS)

FOR THE GRAVY

1 cup (140 g) diced onion

4 oz (120 g) parsnip, peeled and sliced

1 clove garlic, peeled and smashed

½ cup (120 ml) Chicken Broth (page 225)

½ cup (120 ml) coconut milk

1 tbsp (15 ml) bacon fat

½ tsp salt

¼ tsp dried thyme

2 tbsp (30 ml) water

1 tsp arrowroot starch

FOR THE STEAK

¼ cup (30 g) tapioca starch

1 tsp (5 g) salt

½ tsp garlic powder

3 oz (85 g) ground chicken

¾ cup (180 ml) coconut milk

3 tbsp (45 ml) water

8 oz (225 g) plantain chips (see note below)

1½ lbs (680 g) cube steak, cut into portions

Coconut or avocado oil for frying

BLEND: In a saucepan, add the onion, parsnip and garlic. Add the chicken broth and cover the pan with a lid. Bring the liquid to a simmer and cook until the parsnip is fork tender, about 10 minutes. Remove the pan from the heat and pour in the coconut milk, stirring to combine. Add the bacon fat, salt and thyme to the pan. Whisk together the water and arrowroot powder until combined and add to the pan. Use an immersion blender to blend into a smooth gravy. Set the gravy aside and keep warm while you make the chicken fried steak.

SET UP: You will need three bowls large enough to fit the largest piece of cube steak. Combine the tapioca starch, salt and garlic powder in one bowl. Add the ground chicken, coconut milk and water to a high-sided container just wide enough to fit the head of your immersion blender. Blend together until completely smooth and pour into the second bowl. In a food processor, pulse the plantain chips until you have a superfine bread crumb–like dust. Place the plantain crumbs into the third bowl.

BREAD: This is going to work just like the classic breading method. First, dip each piece of cube steak into the starch, gently patting off the excess. Next, dip each piece of cube steak into the coconut milk mixture, making sure both sides are evenly covered. Let any excess liquid drip off the cube steaks. Lastly, dip the cube steaks into the plantain crumbs, making sure to coat both sides and the edges. Transfer the cube steaks to a large plate or cutting board when they are breaded.

FRY: In a large skillet, add enough oil so that the breaded cube steaks will be at least halfway submerged in the oil. Heat the oil over medium-high heat until it starts to shimmer, then carefully drop your breaded cube steaks into the pan—you may need to do this in batches. Cook until the breading is golden brown on both sides, about 6 minutes per side. Serve smothered in the onion gravy and pretend you're at your favorite diner for dinner!

NOTE: Make an unseasoned version of the Crunchy Salad Topper (page 223), to ensure that your plantain chips have been cooked in an AIP friendly fat.

BAKED SWEDISH MEATBALLS
IN GRAVY

Traditional Swedish meatballs are usually pan fried, but baking them the way I do in this recipe is much more efficient: There's no need to stand over the stove supervising batches of meatballs or splattering grease everywhere, plus it saves time because the gravy can be made while the meatballs are baking. The other neat thing about this recipe is that the ingredients used to help bind the meatballs together also form the base of the gravy recipe. Minimal ingredients, maximum flavor—I'm all about that in the kitchen. I couldn't crack this recipe until my friend Peter was kind enough to share some original Swedish meatball recipes...and translate them for me, thankfully! That's when I learned that it is traditional to use potato as a binder, which gave me the final piece of the puzzle for this recipe. These super-tender meatballs have a unique, almost spicy flavor that comes from using plenty of mace as seasoning, plus a lovely richness from the combination of both beef and pork. Thanks, Peter!

SERVES 4

2½ cups (600 ml) Beef Broth (page 224), divided

1 tbsp (7 g) powdered gelatin

2 tsp (10 ml) coconut or avocado oil

¼ cup (35 g) diced onion

½ cup (120 ml) coconut milk

1 cup (240 g) white sweet potato, baked and cooled

½ lb (227 g) ground beef

½ lb (227 g) ground pork

1 tsp (5 g) salt

½ tsp ground mace

BLEND: Pour ½ cup (120 ml) of the beef broth into a bowl and sprinkle the powdered gelatin over it. Set aside to let the gelatin bloom. In a small saucepan over medium heat, add the oil and cook the diced onion until softened. Reduce the heat and pour in the coconut milk. Once the coconut milk in the pan is warm, add the bloomed gelatin to the pan and stir until the gelatin dissolves into the liquid. Remove the saucepan from the heat and pour the liquid into a blender. Add the white sweet potato and 1 cup (240 ml) of beef broth, then blend on high until smooth, scraping down the sides as needed. Take the lid off the blender and let the pureed mixture cool.

BAKE: Line a baking tray with parchment paper. In a mixing bowl, add the beef, pork, salt and mace. Pour ½ cup (120 ml) of the pureed sweet potato mixture over the meat. Don't panic when it looks like there is way too much liquid in the bowl! I promise there isn't: As you begin to mix the meatball mixture together (using your hands is easiest), the liquid will be absorbed. The meatball mixture will be a little softer than normal to work with. Use a 2 tablespoon (30 ml) scoop to divide the mixture into approximately 16 meatballs. With damp hands or while wearing gloves, roll the meatballs and drop them onto the lined baking tray, evenly spaced. Preheat the oven to 400°F (205°C). Put the baking tray of meatballs into the refrigerator to firm up a little while the oven comes to temperature. Bake the meatballs for 20 minutes.

REDUCE: While the meatballs are baking, pour the remainder of the pureed sweet potato mixture from the blender into a skillet large enough to fit all the meatballs in a single layer once they are baked. Add the remaining 1 cup (240 ml) of beef broth to the skillet: This will make the gravy for the meatballs. Bring the gravy to a simmer and cook until thickened enough that you can pull a spatula through the pan without the gravy instantly filling in the gap. As the gravy is cooked it will darken, too. Taste the gravy and add salt, to taste, if needed. Once the gravy is thickened to your liking, add the meatballs to the pan and toss to coat with the gravy and warm through before serving.

NOT CRAZY ABOUT COCONUT? Omit the coconut milk, add an extra 2 tablespoons (30 ml) of Beef Broth and an extra ¼ cup (60 g) of baked sweet potato to the blender.

PORK BELLY CARNITAS
WITH APPLE

Pork and apple is a classic flavor pairing, but you wouldn't necessarily expect it in a carnitas recipe. Here apple juice does double duty as both marinade and cooking liquid, adding a gentle sweetness that contrasts gorgeously with the warm hint of cinnamon. Throw out all those ideas about "healthy" always meaning low-fat! Pastured pork is full of good fatty acids like omega-3s and is a rich source of both vitamin D and E. And where are these great vitamins stored? In the fat! Healthy animals make healthy vitamin-filled fat. What does this mean for you? You can eat ridiculously delicious, crispy-edged Pork Belly Carnitas while nourishing your body at the same time. Yay!

SERVES 4

2 cups (480 ml) unsweetened apple juice

2 tbsp (24 g) garlic powder

2 tbsp (4 g) dried oregano leaves

1 tbsp (15 g) salt (reduce or omit if using broth with salt in it)

2 tsp (2 g) ground cinnamon

1 tsp (2 g) ground sage

4 dried bay leaves

2½ lbs (1.1 kg) skinless pork belly, cut into 1½-inch (4-cm) cubes

2 cups (480 ml) Pork or Chicken Broth (page 225)

MARINATE: In a large container or freezer bag, combine the apple juice, garlic powder, oregano, salt, cinnamon, sage and bay leaves. Add the pork belly pieces and refrigerate while they marinate, for at least 2 hours and up to overnight.

BRAISE: Preheat the oven to 350°F (180°C). Put the pork belly pieces into a large Dutch oven in a single layer, fat-side up. Then pour the marinade over the pork belly. Add the broth to the Dutch oven and cook, covered, for 2 hours. After 2 hours, remove the lid and cook the pork belly for another hour. This will cook off the remaining liquid and finish rendering the pork fat.

FRY: Remove the pork belly from the oven. Remove and discard the bay leaves, then transfer the pork pieces to a large flat-bottomed skillet. Spoon off as much of the fat as you can from the Dutch oven and add it to the skillet with the pork belly pieces. Avoid any solids from the bottom of the Dutch oven as these will burn! Over low-medium heat, continue to cook the pork belly in its own rendered fat. The fat should bubble, but not be so hot that it spits. Flip the pork belly pieces so that they brown evenly on all sides. This should take about 30 minutes. When all sides of the pork belly are brown and crispy, remove them from the pan and drain any excess fat on a paper towel–covered plate. Shred the pork belly carnitas with two forks and enjoy!

PESTO PORK
WITH LITTLENECK CLAMS

I absolutely adore clams. They're naturally sweet, but refreshingly briny at the same time. But since they're sold per pound, most of which is shell, they're not the cheapest source of protein. So to stretch my dollars a little further, I like to pair them with pork. This recipe uses light and fragrant ground pesto pork as a base for the dish—and lets the clams really shine as the highlight. Steaming the clams on top of the pork keeps them out of the steaming liquid without having to mess about with steaming racks—and makes some of the juiciest, most tender clams ever.

SERVES 4

2 lbs (900 g) wild-caught littleneck clams

½ packed cup + 2 tbsp (20 g + 5 g) fresh basil leaves, divided

¼ cup (60 ml) avocado oil

2 cloves garlic, peeled

1 tbsp (15 ml) lemon juice

1 lb (454 g) lean ground pork

1 onion, cut in half and sliced finely

1 cup (240 ml) Seafood Stock or Pork Broth (page 225)

PREP: Rinse the littleneck clams under cold running water and use a stiff brush to get rid of any sand or sediment on the outside of the shells. Put the scrubbed clams into a bowl and cover them with cold water. If any of the clams are open, tap them on the edge of the bowl and see if they close. If they close, they are still alive and edible; any clams that don't close should be discarded. Let the clams sit for 10 minutes, then discard the dirty water and refill the bowl. Let the clams soak while you make the pesto.

MIX: Add ½ cup (20 g) of the basil leaves to a mini food processor, reserving the rest to use as garnish later. Add the avocado oil, garlic and lemon juice, then process until a smooth pesto is formed. In a bowl, mix together the ground pork and pesto until just combined. Discard the water covering the clams, then rinse them a final time. Pop the cleaned clams into the fridge in a bowl while you cook the pork.

COOK: Add the pesto pork to a skillet over medium heat and cook until no longer pink in the middle, breaking up large pieces with the back of a spoon. Use a slotted spoon to transfer the cooked pork to a bowl, leaving behind the juices from the meat. Reduce the heat a little and add the sliced onions to the pan. Cook until they are softened and just beginning to take on a little color at the edges, about 10 minutes. Return the cooked pork to the pan and add the stock or broth. Turn up the heat and bring the liquid to a simmer. Place the clams on top of the pork and onions, then cover the pan with a lid and steam until the clams open and are cooked through, about 5 minutes. Slice the reserved basil into thin strips and scatter over the top and serve immediately.

SLOW COOKER BISON "CHILI"
WITH HIDDEN VEGGIES

This rich and thick "chili" is downright sneaky. It has no tomatoes or, well, chili in it—and yet it is packed with layers of flavor: The richness of the meat meets the umami from the mushrooms and is elevated by the brightness and slight spiciness of the Taco Seasoning. All of these elements come together to make a "chili" that is just as satisfying as the real thing. Since this is made in the slow cooker, it's also super-easy to make—and freezes well, to boot! With almost three pounds (1.3 kg) of vegetables in this recipe, who knew chili could be so healthy?

SERVES 8

---

2 lbs (900 g) ground bison

¼ cup (25 g) Taco Seasoning (page 219), divided

3 cups (420 g) diced onion

¾ lb (340 g) carrots

½ lb (225 g) beets

3 cups (720 ml) Beef Broth (page 224)

¾ cup (180 ml) pumpkin puree

6 oz (175 g) mushrooms

2 tbsp (30 ml) apple cider vinegar

1 tsp (5 g) salt

1½ tbsp (10 g) arrowroot or tapioca starch

Juice of 1 lime

BROWN: In a large skillet over medium heat, work in batches to brown the ground bison. Transfer the browned meat with a slotted spoon to your slow cooker and keep covered. If you need to, pour out any excess fat from the skillet, leaving behind 1 tablespoon (15 ml) to cook the vegetables in. Add the Taco Seasoning to the reserved fat in the skillet and cook until fragrant, about 30 seconds. Add the diced onion to the pan and toss to coat. Use a box grater or the medium shredder blade of your food processor (much less messy!) to coarsely grate the carrots and beets. Add the shredded vegetables to the skillet and toss to combine again. Cover the pan with a lid and cook until the carrots and beets begin to soften, about 10 minutes, stirring a few times as you go so that they don't stick.

BLEND: Once the vegetables are softened, remove the pan from the heat. Transfer about a third of the vegetables to the slow cooker and the rest to a blender. Add the broth, pumpkin puree and mushrooms to the blender with the other vegetables, then blend until smooth. Pour the blended sauce into the slow cooker and add the apple cider vinegar and salt. Stir everything through to combine, then cook on high for 3 hours.

THICKEN: Mix the arrowroot or tapioca starch with a little water to make a paste, then add to the chili in the slow cooker. Add the lime juice to the chili and season to taste with extra salt if needed. Cook on low for another hour to thicken. Here at Meatified HQ, we like our chili thick and chunky. If you like a thinner chili that is closer to a soup, add a little extra broth before you cook the chili for the final hour. Can be eaten straight away, but is best the next day to give the flavors time to marry and develop.

WARM CHICKEN "GRAIN" SALAD
WITH ROASTED BUTTERNUT SQUASH & GREENS

While I do love cauliflower rice, it just doesn't have the right texture to mimic larger grains like those found in warm wintry grain salads. That's what prompted me to come up with the basic recipe for what we nickname "protein rice" here at home! All the flavors of fall—herby "grains," roasted butternut squash and lots of greens—combine here to make a delicious warm salad that will have even non-AIP-ers asking for seconds. Packed with protein and with plenty of calcium coming from the leafy greens, this salad is a winner nutritionally, too.

SERVES 4

4 cups (560 g) butternut squash

2 tsp + 1 tbsp (10 ml + 15 ml) coconut or avocado oil, divided

1 tsp (5 g) salt, divided

1 lb (454 g) ground chicken

1 tsp (4 g) garlic powder

1 tsp (2 g) ground sage

1 tsp dried rosemary leaves

½ cup (70 g) diced onion

8 oz (225 g) Swiss chard

4 oz (115 g) spinach

Squeeze of lemon juice

ROAST: Preheat the oven to 425°F (220°C). Cut the butternut squash into ½-inch (13-mm) cubes and toss with 2 teaspoons (10 ml) of the oil and ½ teaspoon of salt. Line a baking tray with parchment paper and spread the squash out in a single layer. Roast the squash until it is tender and beginning to brown and caramelize at the edges, about 15–20 minutes. Reserve the cooked squash for later.

COOK: Add the remaining 1 tablespoon (15 ml) of oil to a skillet over low-medium heat. When the pan is hot, add the ground chicken, breaking it into a few large pieces with your hands before dropping it into the pan. Don't break up the chicken in the pan any further or it will overcook and become very dry. Sprinkle the remaining ½ teaspoon of salt, garlic powder, sage and rosemary over the chicken and cover the pan with a lid. Cook the chicken, covered, until it is cooked through and there is no pink inside, about 5-6 minutes, turning the chicken over halfway through. Do not overcook the chicken—it should release juices into the pan and still be tender when cooked through. Use a slotted spoon to transfer the cooked chicken to a paper towel-lined plate. Add the diced onion to the pan and cook until softened, about 5 minutes, then remove the pan from the heat.

ASSEMBLE: Crumble the cooked chicken into the bowl of a food processor. Pulse 3–5 times, until the chicken is broken up into little "grains." Do not overprocess, or you will end up with a sticky paste! Finely slice the chard and spinach. Toss together the "grains," roasted squash, chard and spinach back in the pan with the onion and all the pan juices. Squeeze a little lemon juice over the salad, to taste, and toss together to combine. The salad can be eaten straightaway, but also refrigerates nicely so you could make it ahead of time and serve it as a cold "grain" salad, too. When it's warmer, I like to swap the butternut squash for roasted asparagus, beets or summer squash and lighter greens, but the possibilities are almost endless!

LAMB LOIN CHOPS
WITH GARLIC & HERB WHIPPED ARTICHOKE "BUTTER"

These small lamb loin chops are perfect for a quick dinner since they are so quick to cook. Before I stopped eating dairy, I used to love lamb paired with yogurt-based sauces. This is a little play on those recipes, without needing to rely on dairy for creaminess, because the artichoke hearts become rich and fluffy when they're whipped. The garlic, herbs and lemon juice make this dish light and tangy—a perfect balance against the richness of the lamb, without overshadowing its natural flavor.

SERVES 4

2 lbs (900 g) small bone-in lamb loin chops, about 1-inch (2.5-cm) thick

1 tsp (5 g) salt

¼ cup (60 ml) + 1 tbsp (15 ml) avocado oil, divided

4.5 oz (130 g) drained artichoke hearts

1–2 cloves garlic, to taste

1 tbsp (3 g) fresh mint leaves

1 tbsp (3 g) fresh basil leaves

1½ tsp (1 g) fresh thyme leaves

2 tsp (10 ml) lemon juice

1 tbsp (15 ml) reserved pan juices

SEAR: Lay out the lamb chops on a chopping board and sprinkle both sides of them lightly with salt, as well as the layer of fat on the outside ease of the chops. Let the salted chops sit at room temperature for about 15 minutes. Heat a cast-iron skillet on high—and fire up a vent fan if you have one. These need to sear in a screaming-hot pan and will smoke! When the skillet is hot, drop in 1 tablespoon (15 ml) avocado oil and swirl it so that it evenly coats the skillet. Working in batches as needed, put the lamb chops into the pan, fat side down and cook until the fat renders and browns, about 5 minutes. This will give you lots of delicious fat to sear the chops in. Flip the chops over and sear them until browned, about 4–5 minutes per side for medium. Remove the pan from the heat, reserving the cooking juices in the pan, and transfer the chops to a plate to rest while you make the whipped artichokes.

WHIP: If the artichokes are in brine, rinse them before draining to get rid of any excess salt. Add the drained artichokes, along with the remaining avocado oil, to a mini food processor and process until combined. Add the garlic, mint, basil, thyme, lemon juice and the reserved pan juices then process again. Divide the lamb chops between 4 plates and spoon a little of the whipped artichokes on top of each chop.

THAI CHICKEN SOUP
WITH COCONUT MILK

Everybody knows that chicken soup is one of the most comforting things ever—and everybody thinks their mom's/grandma's/own version is the best, of course! My favorite version of chicken soup has always been a creamy version with a boatload of seasoning, Thai style. This soup is made with my AIP version of Thai Green "Curry" Paste (page 202), which gives the same layers of flavor that I used to love, while being gentle on my tummy. It's perfect for when you're feeling a little rundown or want a bowl of something soothing and delicious—the healthy fats from the coconut milk make it super satisfying and the gut-healing broth is an added bonus!

SERVES 4

2 tsp (10 ml) coconut or avocado oil

3 tbsp (45 ml) Thai Green "Curry" Paste (page 202)

4 cups (960 ml) Chicken Broth (page 225)

1 lb (454 g) chicken breast or thighs, sliced thinly

2 cups (480 ml) coconut milk

1 tbsp (15 ml) gluten-free fish sauce

2 tbsp (30 ml) lime juice

4 cups (120 g) fresh spinach leaves

4 green onions, chopped, reserving the green ends for garnish

2 tbsp (5 g) fresh cilantro leaves, roughly chopped

2 tbsp (5 g) fresh basil leaves, roughly chopped

COOK: Add the oil to a saucepan over medium heat. When the oil is hot, add the Thai Green "Curry" Paste and fry for a minute or two. Add the chicken broth to the pan and bring almost to a boil. Reduce the heat to a simmer and add the sliced chicken. Cook for 5 minutes, until the chicken is almost cooked through, then add the coconut milk and fish sauce.

SIMMER: Reduce the heat so that the coconut milk will simmer but not break. When the coconut milk–laced broth is hot, add the lime juice. Taste and adjust seasonings as needed: Add more fish sauce for extra saltiness or more lime juice for sourness if you like.

WILT: Add the spinach leaves and white parts of the chopped green onions. Cook until the spinach has just wilted. Divide the soup between 4 bowls and top with the reserved green onion slices, cilantro and basil leaves.

NOT CRAZY ABOUT COCONUT? Swap the coconut milk for an extra 2 cups (480 ml) of Chicken Broth (page 225).

GRILLED THAI BEEF SKEWERS
WITH PINEAPPLE AND GREEN ONIONS

These Thai-inspired beef skewers make the perfect quick grilling food and can even be broiled if the weather's not on your side. They're packed full of flavor from the Thai "Curry" Paste, with an extra bit of zing from fresh lime juice and coconut aminos. No need to miss nightshade spices when you're chowing down on these bad boys!

SERVES 4

¼ cup (60 ml) Thai "Curry" Paste (page 202)

½ cup (120 ml) coconut milk

2 tbsp (30 ml) coconut aminos

2 tbsp (30 ml) lime juice

1 lb (454 g) sirloin steak, sliced thinly

20 bite-size chunks fresh pineapple (about ¼ of a fresh pineapple)

20 (1-inch [2.5-cm]) pieces green onion (about 5 green onions)

MARINATE: In a bowl, whisk together the Thai "Curry" Paste, coconut milk, coconut aminos and lime juice. Slice the sirloin steak into long strips, about 1-inch (2.5-cm) wide. Put the steak into a bowl or freezer bag and pour over the marinade, tossing the steak to make sure it is coated evenly. Refrigerate and marinate for at least 1 hour. If you are going to use wooden skewers, soak them in cold water now, too.

SKEWER: Remove the steak strips from the marinade and shake off any excess. Thread the beef, pineapple and green onion pieces onto the skewers, alternating the ingredients as you go.

GRILL: Heat an outside grill for high, direct heat or indoor broiler on high. If broiling the skewers indoors, line a baking tray with foil and place the skewers onto the tray, with the tray about 4 inches (10 cm) from the broiler on high. If grilling outside, lay the skewers directly onto the grill. Grill or broil for 3–5 minutes per side, turning once. Serve immediately!

NOT CRAZY ABOUT COCONUT? Swap the coconut milk for avocado oil and replace the coconut aminos with 1 tablespoon (15 ml) of gluten-free fish sauce.

DUCK FAT BURGERS
WITH MANGO & SMOKY AVOCADO SPREAD

Grass-fed beef is much leaner than conventionally raised beef, which means burgers can rapidly become dry and tasteless instead of juicy and delicious. My secret weapon? Duck fat. Not only does it add that much-needed extra fat that lean grass fed beef lacks, it gives a hint of extra smokiness to the patties, even if you cook them on the stovetop rather than an outdoor grill. For extra awesomeness, these burgers are topped with an umami-filled avocado spread that adds even more smoky flavor and topped with fresh mango slices for an element of contrasting sweetness. This combination of muscle-building protein and healthy fats is a winner on all counts.

SERVES 4

1 lb (454 g) grass-fed ground beef

2–3 green onions, minced

½ tsp salt

2 tbsp (30 ml) duck fat, divided

8 leaves butter lettuce

4 slices red onion

¼ cup (60 ml) Smoky Avocado Spread (page 199), chilled

1 mango, peeled and sliced

MIX: Add the ground beef, minced green onion, salt and 1 tbsp (15 ml) of the duck fat into a bowl. Use your hands to mix all the ingredients together until they are just combined and the green onions are evenly distributed. Divide the meat mixture into 4 equal parts and shape into burger patties.

COOK: Heat a large skillet or griddle over medium-high heat. Add the remaining duck fat to the pan and swirl to coat evenly. Cook the burgers in the duck fat until browned and cooked through, about 5 minutes per side. Rest the burgers for a few minutes before plating.

STACK: Put each burger on top of two butter lettuce leaves. Top with the red onion slices and a spoonful of Smoky Avocado Spread. Top the stack with mango slices and revel in the meaty goodness of your meal! Oh, and bring plenty of napkins, you'll need them.

CUBAN STYLE PICADILLO
WITH GREEN OLIVES

This is a Cuban-inspired beef dish that is packed with flavor: Beef is simmered in a vegetable-filled sauce with plenty of rich beef broth and a hint of cinnamon, then finished off with buttery green olives. Picadillo can be served a bunch of different ways: on top of cauliflower "rice" or your favorite mashed root vegetables, on top of salad greens or taco-bowl style, topped with guacamole. However you serve it, this is sure to be a hit! In place of the usual tomato-based sauce, I've used beets and carrots—a sneaky way to get some extra antioxidants and vitamins into a meal.

SERVES 4

1 tbsp (15 ml) coconut or avocado oil

2 cups (210 g) fresh grated beets

1½ cups (180 g) grated carrots

2¼ cups (540 ml) Beef Broth (page 224)

1 tbsp (15 ml) red wine vinegar

1 lb (454 g) ground beef

1 cup (140 g) diced onion

4 cloves garlic, minced

2 bay leaves

2 tsp (2 g) dried oregano leaves

¾ tsp ground cinnamon

½ tsp ground mace

½ cup (75 g) green olives, sliced

BLEND: Add the oil to a large skillet over low-medium heat and cook the grated beets and carrots until softened, about 10–15 minutes. Transfer the cooked vegetables to a blender, along with the beef broth and red wine vinegar. Blend until smooth and reserve for later.

BROWN: Add the ground beef to a large skillet and cook until browned, breaking it up into smaller pieces with the back of a spoon. Use a slotted spoon to transfer the browned beef to a bowl; reserve the beef for later. If there is any excess beef fat in the pan, drain it off now, then add the diced onion and minced garlic. Cook until they are softened, about 5 minutes, then add the beef back to the pan.

SIMMER: Add the bay leaves to the pan and sprinkle the oregano, cinnamon and mace over the meat. Pour over the blended vegetables from earlier and stir through to combine, then reduce the heat to low. Cover the pan and simmer for 15 minutes. Uncover the pan and stir through the sliced green olives, cooking for another 5 minutes. Taste and add extra salt if needed just before serving.

OVEN BAKED RIBS
WITH SWEET AND TANGY BBQ SAUCE

Not everybody has the luxury of being able to grill outside and enjoy that delicious smoke-infused flavor of traditional BBQ. So I came up with this foolproof method of baking ribs in the oven that produces ribs that are just as tender. Doused in my AIP-friendly no-nightshade BBQ sauce, they broil up to sticky, saucy, messy rib perfection.

MAKES 1 RACK OF RIBS

3½ lbs (1.5 kg) rack of pork back ribs

1 tsp (5 g) salt

1 tsp (4 g) garlic powder

½ tsp ground ginger

½ tsp ground sage

¼ tsp dried thyme leaves

¼ cup (60 ml) Pork or Chicken Broth (page 225)

½ cup (120 ml) BBQ Sauce (page 201)

PREP: Pat the ribs dry and put them on a cutting board. Trim your ribs: if there is any gristle at the ends of the bones, cut it off and discard. Flip the ribs over so they are bone-side up. Make a shallow cut across the bone and slide your fingers underneath the translucent membrane until you can get a grip on it. Use a piece of paper towel to hold onto the membrane and pull on it firmly so that it comes off the ribs—discard it and flip the ribs back over so the meaty side is facing up. Mix together the salt, garlic, ginger, sage and thyme. Spread the dry rub evenly over the meat and press into place so that it adheres to the meat. Lay out a sheet of aluminum foil large enough to wrap around the rack of ribs, then place a piece of parchment paper that is the same size on top of the foil. Transfer the ribs to the parchment paper. Wrap the parchment paper and foil together around three sides of the ribs. Carefully pour the broth into the foil and parchment package, then wrap the final side up tightly and place the wrapped ribs on a baking tray.

COOK: Preheat the oven to 225°F (105°C). Bake the ribs for 3 hours, then remove them from the oven. Turn off the oven and preheat the broiler on high, setting the oven rack about 6 inches (15 cm) away from the broiler. Carefully unwrap the ribs—there will be lots of cooking liquid underneath the ribs, which means steam escaping when you open up the foil. Line a second baking tray with foil, then use two sets of tongs to transfer the ribs to it carefully.

BROIL: Baste the ribs with BBQ sauce and broil the ribs for 2–3 minutes. Baste the ribs again and broil for another 2–3 minutes, until the sauce is bubbling. Baste the ribs one last time before slicing up the ribs to serve. Have lots and lots of paper towels for the inevitable messy eaters!

NOTE: This recipe yields ribs that are perfectly tender, but still have a little "bite" and will stay on the bone when they are sliced. If you want fall-off-the-bone ribs, you will need to increase the original cooking time to 4 hours before broiling.

OVEN BAKED CHINESE PORK JERKY
WITH ORANGE AND GINGER

Most people think of beef when it comes to jerky, but that's not the only option. This recipe uses pork infused with Chinese-inspired flavors that lighten up the traditional dried meat snack—without relying on a heavy dose of soy sauce. I've kept this recipe coconut amino–free, too, so it's suitable for almost everyone.

MAKES ABOUT 12 OZ (340 G)

2 lbs (900 g) lean pork, such as tenderloin, sliced ⅛-inch (3-mm) thick (see tips below)

FOR THE MARINADE

¼ cup (60 ml) freshly squeezed orange juice

3 tbsp (45 ml) gluten-free fish sauce

2 tbsp (30 ml) avocado oil

2 tbsp (30 ml) ume plum or white wine vinegar

6 green onions, sliced

1½ tbsp (9 g) ground ginger

1 tbsp (12 g) garlic powder

¾ tsp ground cinnamon

MARINATE: Cut the pork into evenly-sized strips about 1 inch (2.5 cm) wide. Use an immersion blender to combine all the marinade ingredients. Put the sliced pork into a freezer bag and pour the marinade over. Mix the pork and marinade together so that the pork is evenly coated, then seal the bag and put it into a bowl to catch any leaks. Marinate the pork in the refrigerator for at least 3 hours.

COOK: Preheat the oven to 300°F (150°C). Line two baking trays with foil—this is just to catch any marinade that drips. Place two oven-safe wire racks onto the baking trays. Shake any excess marinade from the pork strips and lay them out on the wire racks, making sure none of the pieces are touching each other. Bake for 20 minutes, until the pork is fully cooked and has an internal temperature of at least 140°F (60°C). Don't skip this step! This is how we avoid any bacterial nasties that could potentially cause sickness.

DRY: Reduce the oven temperature to 170°F (75°C)—or the lowest temperature your oven will reach. Bake until the jerky is dry, but still pliable, about 3 hours, rotating the trays half way through the cooking time. Store in an airtight container in the fridge.

TIPS: Make sure to use avocado oil in the marinade. Coconut oil will clump up and solidify in the fridge, which means the marinade won't coat evenly and will fall off.

My butcher will very kindly slice my pork super thin for me. However, if that's not an option for you, the easiest way to slice the pork very thinly is to put it into the freezer for 20–30 minutes to firm up before you slice it with a knife. You can also buy thicker-cut pork and use a meat tenderizer to pound it out thinly. If that's not an option, you can make this jerky with thicker pieces, but you will need to increase both the marinating and drying times: ¼-inch (6-mm) thick pieces will need about 6 hours of drying time.

"PONZU" MARINATED STEAK
WITH DAIKON & GREEN ONION

This is a really great way to prepare an inexpensive cut of beef. The marinade tenderizes the beef so the result is a juicy, delicious umami-laden steak without spending big bucks. Sliced thin, a little goes a long way and makes fantastic leftovers for salads or whatever you choose!

SERVES 6–8

FOR THE "PONZU"

2 tbsp (30 ml) coconut aminos

2 tbsp (30 ml) ume plum vinegar

1 tbsp (15 ml) yuzu or lime juice

2 tsp (10 ml) Chicken Broth (page 225)

1 tsp (5 ml) lemon juice

1 tsp (5 ml) gluten-free fish sauce

FOR THE STEAK

⅓ cup (80 ml) orange juice

2 cloves garlic, minced

2 lbs (900 g) sirloin or flank steak, about 1-inch (2.5 cm) thick

1 tsp (5 ml) coconut or avocado oil

¼ cup (30 g) grated daikon radish

2–3 green onions, sliced, green tops only

MARINATE: In a small bowl, whisk together all the "ponzu" ingredients, then add the orange juice and minced garlic. Place the steak in a freezer bag or bowl and pour the marinade over, making sure the steak is evenly coated. Seal or cover and marinate in the refrigerator for 4 hours, turning the steak halfway through.

SEAR: Take the steak out of the refrigerator 30 minutes prior to cooking. Discard the marinade and pat the steak dry. Rub each side of the steak with coconut oil. Heat a cast-iron skillet on high—you will know it's hot enough if a drop of water evaporates immediately when it touches the skillet. Cook the steak in the hot skillet for 3–4 minutes on each side (for rare steak), then remove it from the heat and transfer to a chopping board to let rest for 10 minutes.

SLICE: Slice the rested steak into thin strips against the grain. Serve immediately, topped with the grated daikon and sliced green onions.

NOT CRAZY ABOUT COCONUT? Omit the coconut aminos and add 1 tablespoon (15 ml) of fish sauce and an extra 1 teaspoon (5 ml) of chicken broth.

PERFECT SLICED ROAST BEEF
WITH HERBS

Finding any kind of lunch or deli meat that is AIP compliant is pretty tough, since nightshades and pepper seem to sneak in everywhere. That's one of the reasons I love this brined roast beef recipe. Instead of brining a beef roast for days in advance, like a traditional corned beef recipe, this method allows you to cook a beef roast from frozen and then brine it afterwards for added juiciness and flavor. It makes delicious sliced beef for lunch boxes, snacks, salads and more. I like to use a small beef round cut because it's inexpensive, makes nice-size slices and is quicker to cook than a larger roast. If I need to make a larger batch, I simply double the recipe and use two roasts instead of one larger piece. This is a great weekend recipe that will prepare you for those weekday lunches ahead!

MAKES ABOUT 1¾ LBS (800 G) OF SLICED BEEF

2 lb (900 g) frozen lean boneless beef roast, such as bottom round

⅓ cup (80 g) kosher salt

1 cup (240 ml) hot filtered water

4 cloves garlic, minced

3 bay leaves

1½ tsp (2 g) dried rosemary leaves

1 tsp (1 g) dried thyme leaves

½ tsp ground oregano

½ tsp ground mace

3 cups (700 ml) cold filtered water

ROAST: Preheat the oven to 190°F (88°C). Line a baking tray with foil—this is just to catch any drips—and place an oven-safe rack onto the tray. Put the frozen beef roast onto the rack and roast until it reaches an internal temperature of 135°F (57°C), about 5 hours. Remove the beef from the oven and rest it while you make the brine.

BRINE: Pour the kosher salt and the hot water into a freezer bag large enough to fit the cooked beef roast. Place the bag into a bowl to stop it spilling over while you add the rest of the seasonings. When the salt has almost entirely dissolved, pour in the cold water. Place the cooked beef roast in the brine and twist the bag shut so that the brine covers the whole roast. Put the bag in a bowl, secure the twisted bag with a clip and seal it shut. Brine the beef roast in the refrigerator for 3 hours.

DRY: Remove the beef from the brine and pat it dry. Wrap the finished beef up and allow it to rest overnight in the refrigerator. Once it has rested overnight, it is ready to be sliced and used however you wish!

NOTE: If you cook the beef to medium-rare, it will let out some additional liquid while it is resting overnight—this isn't anything to worry about! If you prefer your meat a little more well-done, cook the roast to an internal temperature of 140°F (60°C).

(See picture on page 30)

BRAISED SHORT RIBS
WITH PAN GRAVY

These short ribs are definitely a weekend cooking project because of the long cooking time, but they're simple to make and don't require much hands-on time at all. Normally gravies rely on all kinds of flours or starches that need to be avoided on the AIP, but this recipe makes its own gravy simply by blending together the braised vegetables and the juices from the short ribs. The result is a rich, decadent dish from a few simple ingredients: You won't miss normal gravy at all!

SERVES 8

6 lbs (2.7 kg) bone-in short ribs

¼ cup (60 ml) coconut or avocado oil, divided

2 onions, diced

2 carrots, diced

6 cloves garlic, minced

4 cups (960 ml) Beef Broth (page 224)

6 sprigs fresh rosemary

Salt, to taste

SEAR: In a large skillet, in batches as needed, sear the short ribs in 3 tablespoons (45 ml) of the oil over medium heat. Cook for 2–3 minutes per side, until nicely browned. Once all the short ribs have been browned, set them aside in a large, high-sided roasting pan.

BRAISE: Preheat the oven to 325°F (163°C). Add the remaining oil to the skillet and soften the onions and carrots, about 5 minutes. Add the minced garlic and cook until fragrant, about 1 minute. Remove the vegetables from the heat and transfer them to the roasting pan, laying them in between the short ribs. Pour over the beef broth and tuck the rosemary sprigs into the pan. Cover the roasting pan with foil and make a hole in the foil for steam to escape. Place the roasting pan in the oven and cook for 3 hours covered, turning the short ribs once halfway through. Remove the foil and cook uncovered for an additional hour to brown and reduce the pan juices, turning the short ribs halfway through the cooking time.

PUREE: Remove the roasting tray from the oven. Remove the short ribs from the pan and let them rest while making the pan gravy. Remove and discard the rosemary stems. Use an immersion blender to puree together the vegetables and liquid in the pan to make the gravy. If you like a thinner gravy, add a little extra broth. Season to taste with salt. Serve the short ribs smothered with gravy and tuck in!

PASTITSIO PIE
WITH CREAMY "BÉCHAMEL" SAUCE

I'll be honest, this is about as much a pie as shepherd's pie is, in that it is topped with vegetables rather than crust. But it is ridiculously delicious, so I don't think you'll hold the crustlessness against me! The traditional Greek dish is a cinnamon-spiked lamb filling with pasta and a rich béchamel sauce, but my version shows that you don't need the pasta to create a dish with pizzazz! I've kept the warmly spiced lamb and created my own twist on a creamy sauce using butternut squash to replace the traditional dairy. This is a family-friendly meal with hidden vegetables, and a great recipe to keep in your arsenal.

SERVES 8

FOR THE MEAT FILLING
1 tsp coconut or avocado oil

2 lbs (900 g) lean ground lamb

1½ cups (210 g) diced onion

2 cloves garlic, minced

2 tsp (2 g) ground cinnamon

1 tsp (1 g) dried oregano leaves

½ tsp ground thyme

1 tsp (5 g) salt

¾ cup (180 ml) Beef Broth (page 224), divided

1 cup (240 ml) coconut milk

1 cup (240 ml) pumpkin puree

2 cups (60 g) fresh spinach leaves

FOR THE SAUCE
12 oz (340 g) peeled and chopped butternut squash

¾ cup (180 ml) coconut milk

1 clove garlic

⅛ tsp ground mace

BROWN: In a large skillet, add the oil and, working in batches, brown the ground lamb until just cooked through. Remove all but a tablespoon (15 ml) of rendered fat from the skillet. Add the diced onion to the skillet and cook over low-medium heat until the onion has softened. Break up any large lumps in the ground lamb with the back of a spoon or spatula.

SIMMER: Add the minced garlic to the meat mixture in the pan, as well as the cinnamon, oregano, thyme and salt. Cook until the garlic and herbs are fragrant, then add ½ cup (120 ml) of the beef broth. Simmer until the broth has reduced and add the coconut milk to the pan. Reduce the heat and simmer until the liquid in the pan has reduced and the lamb is lightly coated. Add the pumpkin puree and remaining beef broth, cooking until warmed through and combined, about 5 minutes. Stir through the spinach and remove from the heat.

ASSEMBLE: Add all the sauce ingredients to a high-power blender and blend until smooth, seasoning to taste with salt if needed. Preheat the oven to 350°F (175°C). Spoon the meat filling into a 9x13-inch (23x33-cm) baking dish and press down on the filling with the back of a spoon to level the top. Place the baking dish on a baking tray, then pour the sauce over the top of the meat mixture. Bake until the filling is piping hot and the surface of the sauce has just set, about 35 minutes. Rest the pie for 5 minutes before serving.

NOT CRAZY ABOUT COCONUT? Leave out the coconut milk from the meat filling and add an extra ¼ cup (60 ml) of pumpkin puree and an extra ½ cup (120 ml) of beef broth. Omit the coconut milk from the sauce and add 2 tablespoons (30 ml) of avocado oil and ¼ cup (60 ml) of additional beef broth.

GLAZED & BAKED CHICKEN WINGS
WITH MANGO AND LIME

Most chicken wing recipes are either slathered in processed sugar or doused in hot sauce. Neither of those options is exactly AIP friendly. I'm getting a stomachache just thinking about them. Thankfully, there is another way! My version of chicken wings have a secret fruit ingredient that most people can't guess—mango. The natural sugars help create that caramelized glaze but don't interfere with the flavor coming from a combination of coconut aminos, fish sauce and plenty of fresh garlic and ginger. These wings are perfect for game day, parties or potlucks!

SERVES 8

6 cloves garlic, peeled

12 oz (340 g) mango peeled, pitted & cubed

¼ cup (60 ml) fresh lime juice (about 2 limes)

¼ cup + 2 tbsp (90 ml) coconut aminos

¼ cup (60 ml) coconut or avocado oil

¼ cup (60 ml) (or more) water

3 tbsp (20 g) minced ginger

1 tbsp (15 ml) gluten-free fish sauce

Zest of 2 limes

6 lbs (2.7 kg) chicken wings

MARINATE: Add all of the ingredients (except the chicken wings!) to a blender and process until combined. In a large freezer bag or container, pour the marinade over the chicken wings and toss to coat them evenly. If the marinade is a little thick, add an extra splash or two of water. Marinate the wings for at least 30 minutes.

PREP: Preheat the oven to 400°F (205°C). Line two baking trays with foil. Place an oven-safe wire rack on each tray. Divide the chicken wings evenly between the two trays. Shake off any excess marinade and lay the wings on top of the wire racks.

BAKE: Cook the chicken wings for 30 minutes. Remove the wings from the oven and use tongs to turn them over. Turn the oven up to 425°F (220°C). Return the wings to the oven and continue to bake until golden-brown, about 10 minutes.

NOTE: Frozen mango chunks work perfectly in the marinade. I find I get the best crisping results in a convection oven. If your wings are not crisped to your liking after cooking, pop them under a broiler to finish up for a few minutes.

NOT CRAZY ABOUT COCONUT? Omit the coconut aminos and add another 2 tablespoons (30 ml) of avocado oil, as well as an additional 2 tablespoons (30 ml) of fish sauce.

STEAK FAJITAS
WITH GRILLED ONIONS, NOPALES AND SUMMER SQUASH

Typical fajitas are filled with AIP no-no ingredients like peppers and chili. This recipe shows you how to make a flavorful and tender steak marinade without nightshades or seed spices that is just perfect for fajitas. Swapping the usual grilled peppers for nopales, or cactus paddles, adds a little extra Mexican flair and a lovely bright fresh citrus flavor to the vegetables, too!

SERVES 4-6

2 lbs (900g) skirt steak

½ cup + 2 tbsp (120 ml + 30 ml) avocado oil, divided

3 tbsp (18 g) Taco Seasoning (page 219)

⅓ cup (80 ml) fresh lime juice

1 tsp (5 g) salt

2 red onions

4 nopales/cactus paddles

2 yellow summer squash

TIP: Avocado oil remains liquid when refrigerated, while coconut oil solidifies, which is why this recipe uses avocado oil—cold, clumping coconut oil doesn't sear evenly. If you do use coconut oil, bring the marinated skirt steaks up to room temperature first so that the marinade is evenly distributed across the surface of the meat.

MARINATE: Prep your skirt steak by trimming off any excess fat from the surface. You don't need to trim off every last bit of fat, just the thick outer layer so that the meat is exposed—there should still be nice layers of fat throughout the meat itself. If you see any membrane left behind, pull that off, too. Cut the skirt steak into 4 evenly sized pieces—this just makes it easier to handle. Whisk together ½ cup (120 ml) of the avocado oil with the Taco Seasoning, lime juice and salt. Place the skirt steak pieces into a freezer bag and pour the marinade over—make sure that each side of the meat is evenly coated, then refrigerate and marinate for 1–3 hours before cooking.

SEAR: You can cook your steaks on a super-hot cast-iron griddle on the stovetop, or on the grill—whichever you prefer. Remove the steak pieces from the marinade and shake off any excess. Sear them on the hot griddle or grill until the outside has a great deep-colored crust and the internal temperature of the meat is about 120°F (49°C) for medium rare or 130°F (54°C) for medium: about 3–5 minutes per side. Set the seared steaks aside on a chopping board to rest while you get the vegetables ready.

PREP: Cut the onions in half and discard the skin, then slice them about ¼-inch (6-mm) thick. Carefully pick up the nopales—it is possible to buy them with the thorns already removed, but handle them carefully, just in case! If you need to remove the thorns, carefully cut around the side and base of the cactus paddle, discarding the edges. Then use the flat of your knife to cut off the thorns from both sides of the paddles. Discard those sharp bits! Slice the nopales diagonally across into strips the same thickness as the onions. Trim the summer squash ends, then slice them in half lengthwise. Cut the summer squash halves into half moons, about the same thickness as the other vegetables. Add the sliced onions to a bowl with the remaining 2 tablespoons (30 ml) of the avocado oil.

GRILL: Heat a cast-iron skillet on the stovetop or grill—it needs to be hot enough that the vegetables sizzle as soon as they're added to the pan. Once the pan is hot enough, shake the excess oil from the onions and add them to the pan. Cook until they begin to soften, stirring occasionally. Toss the summer squash in the remaining oil—once the onions have begun to color, add the squash to the pan and cook until they just begin to soften, about 3 minutes. Add the sliced nopales to the pan and cook until they are tender-crisp and bright green, about 2 more minutes.

SERVE: Remove the vegetables from the heat and pile them onto a large platter. Slice the rested steak into strips against the grain and add to the platter. Pour any steak juices over the veggies. Let everybody make up their own plates from the shared platter and serve the fajitas with extra lime wedges.

LAMB & LEEK BURGERS
WITH LEMON "CREAM"

Most people reach for beef when it comes to burgers, but there are plenty of reasons to swap that for some ground lamb instead. It has a more robust flavor than beef that really works well with burgers or grilled recipes. Here I paired the lamb with another springtime ingredient: leeks. The natural sweetness of slightly caramelized leeks makes a nice, simple twist on the classic beef burger. Ground lamb is the cheapest way to get the nutritional benefits of grass-fed lamb, which include being a fabulous source of protein, having plenty of good-for-us omega-3 fatty acids *and* being a great source of conjugated linoleum acid (CLA), which is another significant anti-inflammatory fatty acid. So...go, team lamb!

MAKES 4 BURGERS

FOR THE BURGERS
1 cup (45 g) leeks, washed and chopped

1 tbsp (15 ml) coconut or avocado oil, divided

1 lb (454 g) ground lamb

½ tbsp (6 g) garlic powder

½ tsp salt

FOR THE "CREAM"
½ cup (120 ml) coconut cream

1 tbsp (5 g) lemon zest

MIX: Add the chopped leeks and half of the coconut oil to a pan and cook over low-medium heat until the leeks are softened, about 5 minutes. Transfer the leeks to a bowl and chill them in the refrigerator. To a second bowl, add the ground lamb, garlic powder and salt. Once the leeks are no longer hot to the touch, add them to the bowl with the meat and use your hands to gently combine the mixture. Divide into 4 evenly-sized patties.

COOK: Add the remaining oil to a skillet. Over medium heat, add the patties and cook each side until browned, about 5 minutes per side, making sure the lamb is cooked all the way through. Rest the burgers while you make the lemon cream.

CREAM: In a bowl, stir together the coconut cream and lemon zest. Use to top the cooked burgers just before serving.

NOT CRAZY ABOUT COCONUT? Try topping with ½ cup (115 ml) of Spinach Artichoke Dip (page 209), instead.

THE ULTIMATE LIVER HATER'S PÂTÉ
WITH APPLE AND THYME

Liver is a superfood in its own right, since it's one of the best sources of vitamin A and contains plenty of vitamin B12, not to mention minerals that we need, like selenium, potassium and zinc, just to name a few. Most people aren't falling over themselves to eat it, though, because it's so easy to overcook—and so often is overcooked! Mr. Meatified was a resolute liver-hater after a childhood of dubiously prepared liver and onions. This pâté, though? It's a game changer. This is the pâté that got him to realize that liver can be decadent and delicious! This recipe has a creamy, whipped texture and extra flavor from using both bacon and bacon fat to make it so smooth. Add in the subtle sweetness from the apple and a little herb-y hit from the thyme and you've got an addictive spread! Try this recipe on your very own liver-haters. And if you want to be extra sneaky...slowly increase the amount of liver in the recipe until you are making it with up to a pound (454 g) of liver. They'll never know!

MAKES AT LEAST 1½ CUPS (360 ML)

½-1 lb (225-454 g) chicken livers

4 oz (115 g) bacon (about 4 slices)

2 shallots, chopped

1 apple, peeled, cored and chopped

1 tbsp (2 g) fresh thyme

1 tsp (1 g) dried rosemary leaves

2 tbsp (30 ml) Chicken Broth (page 225)

¼ cup (60 ml) bacon fat

COOK: Trim the chicken livers of any fat or connective tissue, then refrigerate until needed. Chop the bacon finely and add to a skillet over medium heat. Cook the bacon until it begins to brown, then reduce the heat a little and add the chopped shallots, apple, thyme and rosemary. Cook until the shallots and apples have softened, about 10 minutes. Add the chicken livers to the pan and cook for a few minutes, turning so that each side browns but the inside remains a little pink. Transfer everything from the skillet to a blender. Return the skillet to the heat and add the chicken broth. Bring to a boil and scrape up any browned pieces from the pan, then pour the broth into the blender, too. Puree on high until the pâté is completely smooth, then add the bacon fat and blend together.

CHILL: Spoon the pâté into mason jars or ramekins and chill overnight. Serve with apple slices and your favorite salad vegetables.

PORK SHOULDER
WITH ROASTED GRAPE SAUCE

I love one pot dishes and this one is fantastic. Roasting the pork on top of the black grapes creates the base for a sauce that tastes incredibly rich but only has a few ingredients. The grape sauce gives a similar depth of flavor to a red wine sauce, without having to use (and cook off) alcohol.

SERVES 4

3½ lbs (1.6 kg) bone-in pork shoulder (see note)
2 tbsp (30 ml) bacon fat
2 tsp (8 g) garlic powder
2 tsp (4 g) ground sage
1 tsp (5 g) salt
1 lb 6 oz (624 g) black or red grapes
1 cup (140 g) diced onion
3 sprigs fresh rosemary
10 sprigs fresh thyme
2 tbsp (30 ml) balsamic vinegar
1 tsp (2 g) arrowroot powder

SEAR: Pat the pork shoulder dry. Mix together the bacon fat, garlic, sage and salt in a small bowl. Rub the pork shoulder on both sides with the fat and seasoning mixture. Heat a Dutch oven over medium heat. Sear the pork shoulder until it browns, about 3–5 minutes per side. Set the pork shoulder aside on a plate for now.

ROAST: Preheat the oven to 325°F (163°C). Add a splash of water to the Dutch oven to scrape up the fond, then place the grapes, onion, rosemary and thyme in the bottom. Place the seared pork shoulder on top and cover it with a lid. Roast the pork until the internal temperature reaches 135°F (57°C), about 45 minutes. Once cooked, let the pork shoulder rest while you make the sauce and transfer the Dutch over to the stovetop.

REDUCE: Remove the herb sprigs from the Dutch oven and add the balsamic vinegar. Use an immersion blender to puree the fruit into a sauce. Cook over medium heat so that the sauce simmers and thickens, about 10–15 minutes. Mix the arrowroot powder with a little water until smooth. Remove the fruit sauce from the heat and stir through the arrowroot mixture. To serve, slice the pork shoulder thinly. Pile up your plates with pork, drizzle with roasted grape sauce and enjoy!

NOTE: This recipe works best with a pork shoulder cut about 1-2 inches (2.5-5 cm) thick. You can use thicker pieces, but you will need to increase the cooking time.

CRISPY BEEF TONGUE WRAPS
WITH HERBED HORSERADISH SAUCE

The first time I ate tongue, I was totally shocked. I was expecting something lean and kind of dry: In reality, it is some of the richest and most delicious beef you will ever eat. Seriously! Traditionally, tongue is boiled for a long time to tenderize the meat, but I didn't want to watch over a pot for a few hours. So I came up with an easy slow-cooker method instead. Once the beef tongue is shredded, it's crisped up and fried with onions for a little extra sweetness. This wrap is a perfect way to enjoy the meat: the slight bitterness of the collard greens is a great contrast and adding some extra zing from the herbed horseradish sauce cuts the richness of the meat beautifully. You can actually follow the first step of this recipe and then refrigerate the meat for future meals, which is what I do: I slow-cook the tongue over the weekend and then whip up this quick meal during the week. Yay for batch cooking ahead!

SERVES 4

2 cups (480 ml) Beef Broth (page 224)

2½ lbs (1.1 kg) beef tongue

2 onions, divided

2 tsp (10 g) salt

3 tbsp (45 ml) coconut or avocado oil, divided

½ cup (120 ml) Horseradish Sauce (page 218)

1 tbsp (2 g) fresh thyme leaves

1½ tbsp (1 g) fresh chopped tarragon

1 tsp (4 g) garlic powder

8 fresh collard green leaves

SLOW-COOK: Pour the broth into the bottom of a large slow cooker. Place the tongue in the broth. Slice one of the onions into chunks and add to the broth, too. Sprinkle the beef tongue with the salt. Pop the lid on the slow cooker and cook the tongue on high for 8 hours. Carefully transfer the cooked tongue to a chopping board and allow to cool enough to handle. Use a knife to make a cut into the meat through the skin, then carefully peel off the skin and discard it. Use two forks to shred the meat and reserve it for later.

CRISP: Heat a large skillet over medium heat and add 1 tablespoon (15 ml) of the oil. Slice the remaining onion in half and then into thin slices. Toss the sliced onion in the oil and cook until the edges begin to caramelize, stirring occasionally, about 10 minutes. Remove the onion from the pan and reserve for later. Increase the heat to medium-high and add the remaining oil to the pan. When the oil is hot and shimmering, add the shredded beef tongue, spreading it across the pan in an even layer, pressing it flat with the back of a spatula. Cook until the beef begins to crisp and brown in the oil, then flip over to the other side and repeat. It should take 3–4 minutes per side to crisp up. Toss the shredded beef one more time and cook for another 3–4 minutes, until there are lots of crispy edges on the beef. Add the onions back to the pan and stir through. Remove the pan from the heat and allow the meat to cool slightly, enough to handle the wraps.

ASSEMBLE: Make the herbed horseradish sauce first, stirring the thyme, chopped tarragon and garlic powder through the horseradish sauce. Remove and discard the tough lower stems of the collard greens that don't have any greens attached to them. Use a paring knife to carefully shave off most of the middle stems so that they are about the same thickness as the leaves: This will make them much easier to roll. Lay two collard greens so that they overlap each other in the middle. Spread a little of the horseradish sauce over the leaves, then divide the crispy beef evenly between "wraps," leaving enough room for the leaves to be wrapped around the filling. Fold the edges of the collard green leaves lengthwise over the filling until they overlap in the middle, then roll the leaves from the bottom edge, making a burrito-like "wrap."

ROSEMARY FLATBREAD
WITH PROSCIUTTO & PLUMS

I don't know about you, but one of the things I used to love about a good flatbread was the slightly chewy texture. If you've made any grain-free versions, you'll probably know what I mean when I say: they're so often like giant crackers. Not that I have anything against grain-free crackers...but they're for dip. Sorry, crackers. This flatbread isn't brittle and won't shatter when you bite into it. Then I went overboard and loaded it up with peppery arugula, salty prosciutto and sweet plums. You're welcome!

SERVES 2-4

1 cup (120 g) tapioca starch

¼ packed cup (40 g) coconut flour, sifted

1 tsp (5 g) salt

2 tsp (2 g) dried rosemary leaves

11 oz (310 g) peeled and chopped plantains (about 2)

¼ cup (60 ml) coconut or avocado oil

4 oz (110 g) arugula

2 tbsp (30 ml) extra-virgin olive oil

½ tbsp (8 ml) lemon juice

6 slices of prosciutto

4 plums, sliced thinly

MIX: Preheat the oven to 375°F (190°C) and put a baking tray into the oven on the center rack. In a mixing bowl, add the tapioca starch, coconut flour, salt and rosemary, stirring to combine. In a food processor or high-power blender, combine the chopped plantains and oil, processing until smooth. Pour the plantain batter into the mixing bowl with the dry ingredients and use a spatula to combine into a dough. You should be able to press on the dough without the edges cracking—if it's a little dry, add a little water.

BAKE: Lay out a piece of parchment paper the size of your baking tray and place the dough in the middle. Gently press down on the dough with your hands, stretching it out until it is about ¼-inch (6-mm) thick. Carefully transfer the parchment paper and dough to the hot baking sheet. Bake until the edges of the flatbread are just beginning to brown, about 20 minutes. Remove from the oven and transfer the flatbread to a chopping board.

TOP: Toss the arugula in a bowl with the olive oil and lemon juice. Top the flatbread with the dressed arugula, followed by the prosciutto slices and finally the sliced plums. Cut into slices and serve while still warm.

TIP: The dough works best with plantains that are beginning to ripen. They should be yellow with a few black spots and just a hint of green at the tips.

LOADED SWEET POTATOES
WITH BBQ CHICKEN AND "CHEESE" SAUCE

I'm not going to lie, I was totally thinking about nachos when I came up with this recipe. Since traditional nachos are laden with nightshades, that wasn't really going to work out for me. But you know what *would* work? BBQ nachos! All I needed was to spice up some already baked and shredded chicken with my 100 percent AIP-friendly BBQ sauce! Instead of engaging in fiddly and time consuming chip-making, I decided to bake up some sweet potatoes. And instead of using a gut-punching "cheez" product, I made my own sweet-potato "cheese" sauce to drizzle over the top, flavored with nutritional yeast for a savory kick. The end result is pure comfort food!

SERVES 4

2 lbs (900 g) sweet potatoes (about 2 large)

3 cups (300 g) cooked and shredded chicken

1½ cups (360 ml) BBQ Sauce (page 201)

¼ cup (60 ml) water

¼ cup (60 ml) coconut milk

¼ cup (60 ml) Chicken Broth (page 225)

2 tbsp (8 g) nutritional yeast flakes

1 tbsp (15 ml) avocado oil

½ tsp salt

¼ tsp garlic powder

4 green onions, sliced

¼ packed cup (10 g) fresh cilantro leaves, chopped

BAKE: Preheat the oven to 425°F (220°C). Scrub the sweet potatoes with a brush and pat dry. Line a baking tray with parchment paper or foil. Carefully poke the sweet potatoes with a knife a few times on each side, then place them on the baking tray. Bake until the sweet potatoes are just tender, about 45 minutes, then remove them from the oven and keep them warm.

SAUCE: Add the shredded chicken to a saucepan with the BBQ Sauce and water. Warm the BBQ chicken through over a low-medium heat, stirring occasionally, while you make the "cheese" sauce.

BLEND: Cut the sweet potatoes in half, then scoop a little out of each half until you have ½ cup (120 g) of cooked sweet potato reserved and each of the potatoes has a nice hollow you can load up with filling later. Add the reserved sweet potato to a food processor or blender. Add the coconut milk, chicken broth, nutritional yeast, avocado oil, salt and garlic powder. Blend until you have a thick, smooth and pourable "cheese" sauce. Top the sweet potato halves with the warmed BBQ chicken, then drizzle with the "cheese" sauce. Finish off with the sliced green onions and chopped cilantro, then dig in!

NOT CRAZY ABOUT COCONUT? To make this coconut-free, omit the coconut milk and add an extra tablespoon (15 ml) of avocado oil and an extra 2 tablespoons (30 ml) of chicken broth when making the "cheese" sauce. Follow the instructions for making the Sweet & Tangy BBQ Sauce coconut-free (page 201).

BRAISED SPRING CHICKEN
WITH ARTICHOKES & OLIVES

This dish is full of my favorite things: crispy-skinned chicken, leeks, artichokes and olives. It's spring in a pan! Adding in the white sweet potatoes keeps the chicken out of the sauce so that the skin stays crispy and makes this an easy family-friendly, one-pot meal! It even makes its own pan sauce.

SERVES 6

1 tbsp (15 ml) coconut or avocado oil

3½ lbs (1.6 kg) bone-in chicken leg quarters (about 6)

2 medium leeks, white and pale-green parts only

1 lb (454 g) white sweet potato, peeled and chopped into bite-size pieces

7 oz (200 g) quartered artichoke hearts

¾ cup (110 g) kalamata olives in olive oil, drained (see Note)

2 cloves garlic, peeled and minced

Juice and zest of one lemon

1 tbsp (5 g) fresh minced sage

½ tsp salt

¾ cup (180 ml) Chicken Broth (page 225)

Handful of fresh basil, cut into strips

BROWN: In a large skillet over medium-high heat, add the oil. In batches, place the chicken leg quarters skin-side down in the pan and cook until the skins are browned and some of the fat has rendered. Put the chicken aside, skin-side up, while you get the rest of the dish ready for the oven. Reserve the pan juices.

BRAISE: Preheat the oven to 425°F (220°C). Slice the leeks finely and chop the sweet potato into bite-size pieces. Put the leeks, white sweet potato, artichoke hearts, olives, garlic, lemon juice and zest, sage and salt into a large 4.8-quart (4.5-liter) baking dish. Add 2 tablespoons (30 ml) of the reserved pan juices and toss the vegetables to coat. Pour over the chicken broth and cook for 30–35 minutes, until a thermometer inserted into the thickest part of the chicken reads 165°F (74°C). Stir through the fresh basil and serve the chicken legs with the roasted vegetables, drizzled with the pan sauce.

NOTE: You can use olives that come in a brine—just rinse them to remove extra salt before adding them to the dish.

QUICK BEEF NOODLE BOWL
WITH SHIITAKE MUSHROOMS

Good broth is so nourishing and soothing...but this bowl upgrades broth to comfort-food status, jammed full of flavor from rich beef, shiitake mushrooms and plenty of aromatics. Extra fun and slurp factor comes from finishing the bowl with zucchini noodles!

SERVES 4

2 tsp (10 ml) coconut or avocado oil

½ onion

4-inch (10-cm) piece peeled ginger root

6 garlic cloves

1 cinnamon stick

2 whole dried cloves

8 cups (1.9 liters) Beef Broth (page 224)

½ oz (15 g) dried shiitake mushrooms

4 zucchini

1 lb (454 g) beef sirloin

1 tbsp (15 ml) gluten-free fish sauce

AS GARNISH

½ onion

2 limes

Fresh cilantro leaves

Fresh basil leaves

Fresh mint leaves

Green onions

INFUSE: In a saucepan, heat the oil over low-medium and add the onion half, cut-side down. Cut the ginger into slices and add to the pan. Peel the garlic and lightly smash the cloves with the back of a knife, then add those to the pan, too. Cook until the ginger and garlic are softened, about 5 minutes, then add the cinnamon stick and cloves. Pour in the beef broth and turn the heat up, bringing to a simmer. Keep at a simmer for 30 minutes to infuse the broth with flavor.

PREP: While the broth is infusing, soak the shiitake mushrooms in just enough hot water to cover them. Peel the zucchini, then use a mandoline, spiralizer or julienne peeler to make long strips of zucchini to act as "noodles." Reserve those in the fridge for later. Slice the beef thinly against the grain and pop the sliced beef in the fridge, too. Thinly slice the onion, quarter the limes and roughly chop the cilantro, basil, mint and green onions. Set out the garnishes in bowls or on a platter for people to choose their own soup toppings.

FINISH: Use a slotted spoon to remove the onion, ginger, garlic, cinnamon and cloves from the broth and discard. Add the mushrooms along with the soaking liquid, as well as the fish sauce to the still-simmering broth. Divide the zucchini "noodles" and thinly sliced beef between 4 bowls and ladle the hot broth over the top—the beef will cook through in the broth. Allow everybody to top their "noodle" bowls as they wish before serving.

CHICKEN CURRY
WITH CREAMY SPICED PUMPKIN

Traditional curry is laden with ingredients that we need to avoid on the AIP. I'm looking at you, seed-based spices and nightshades! Instead, this recipe mimics the warmth of a mild curry by building flavor with ginger, cinnamon and turmeric. The turmeric in the spice blend and marinade does more than add color—it's a natural anti-inflammatory. Pumpkin puree thickens the curry without any need for dairy and adds a touch of sweetness, not to mention a nutritional boost because of its high vitamin A content. In fact, each serving of this Pumpkin Chicken Curry has over 200 percent of the recommended daily allowance of vitamin A!

SERVES 4–6

FOR THE MARINADE

⅓ cup (80 ml) coconut cream

4 garlic cloves, minced

2 tbsp (30 ml) lime juice

1 tsp (2 g) ground turmeric

1 tsp (2 g) ground ginger

1 tsp (5 g) salt

FOR THE CURRY

1½ lbs (680 g) boneless skinless chicken thighs

1 tbsp (15 ml) coconut or avocado oil, divided

1 cup (140 g) dried onion

4 cloves garlic, minced

1 tbsp (6 g) fresh ginger, minced

2 tsp (4 g) ground ginger

2 tsp (4 g) ground turmeric

2 tsp (2 g) dried oregano leaves

1 tsp (1 g) ground cinnamon

15 oz (425 g) pumpkin puree

13.5 oz (400 ml) coconut milk

2 tsp (10 ml) lime juice

1 tsp (5 g) salt

2 bay leaves

MARINATE: Mix all the marinade ingredients together in a baking dish or freezer bag. Add the chicken thighs and coat evenly in the marinade. Marinate in the refrigerator for an hour or as long as overnight.

BROWN: Heat ½ tablespoon (7 ml) of coconut oil in a skillet at medium heat. Remove the marinated chicken from the refrigerator and shake off any excess marinade. Place the chicken thighs in the hot pan and cook until each side is browned, about 5 minutes per side. Remove the chicken thighs from the pan and rest them on a plate while you make the curry.

SIMMER: Add the remaining oil to the skillet over low-medium heat and scrape up any pieces of chicken left behind in the pan. Add the onion and cook until softened, about 5 minutes. Stir in the minced garlic and fresh ginger. Cook for 1 minute. Combine the ground ginger, turmeric, oregano leaves and cinnamon with the softened onion, garlic and ginger. Cook for a minute or so, until fragrant. Stir in the pumpkin puree and coconut milk—keep stirring until the sauce is evenly combined, then add the lime juice, salt and bay leaves. Simmer until the sauce is hot and beginning to thicken. Chop the rested chicken thighs into bite-size pieces and add them back to the sauce, along with any meat juices from the plate. Simmer until the chicken is cooked through and the sauce is thickened to taste. Remove the bay leaves before serving.

NOT CRAZY ABOUT COCONUT? Substitute ¼ cup (60 ml) of avocado oil for the coconut cream in the marinade. Replace the coconut milk in the curry sauce with 1 cup (240 ml) of Chicken Broth (page 225).

LAMB LETTUCE CUPS
WITH CUCUMBER SAUCE

I love lamb and it goes perfectly with Greek-inspired flavors. I wanted to make a sauce that could stand in for the traditional tzatziki. Without dairy and without relying on coconut products for creaminess, this cucumber sauce fits the bill and is super simple to whip up! This is a great recipe to have on hand for quick weeknight meals, especially since you can make and refrigerate the sauce in advance.

SERVES 4

FOR THE SAUCE

1 cup (150 g) English cucumber

¼ cup (60 g) mashed avocado

1 tbsp (15 ml) olive oil

1 tbsp (15 ml) lemon juice

1 tsp (1 g) dried dill leaves

FOR THE LAMB

2 tsp (10 ml) coconut or avocado oil

1 cup (140 g) diced onion

3 cloves garlic, minced

1 lb (454 g) ground lamb

2 tsp (2 g) dried oregano leaves

1 tsp (1 g) dried thyme leaves

½ tsp salt

¼ tsp ground cinnamon

⅛ tsp ground mace

1 tbsp (15 ml) lemon juice

Lettuce leaves, to serve

BLEND: Peel the cucumber and scrape out the seeds. Add all of the sauce ingredients to a food processor and blend until smooth. Place a fine-mesh sieve over a bowl and pour the cucumber sauce into the sieve. Put the bowl and sieve in the fridge for the sauce to chill, for about 15 minutes. This will help remove any excess water from the sauce, making it thicker and creamier.

SEASON: Add the oil to a large skillet over medium-low heat. Add the onion and cook for about 5 minutes, then add the garlic and cook for another minute. Add the ground lamb to the pan and cook until browned. Strain off all but 1 tablespoon (15 ml) of rendered fat from the pan. Add the oregano, thyme, salt, cinnamon, mace and lemon juice to the pan, stirring to coat the meat, then cook for another minute or so.

ASSEMBLE: Spoon the seasoned lamb mixture into lettuce cups to serve, then top with cucumber sauce before serving.

CHICKEN & BACON BITES
WITH GREEN ONION AND SAGE

It turns out that the answer to the problem of tasteless, dry chicken burgers, like so many problems in the kitchen, is to add bacon. Adding bacon gives a lovely smoky flavor and creates a super-juicy chicken burger. I love how the green onions lighten up the burger, cutting through the richness and making these burger bites super flavorful and fresh tasting. Choose the best-quality bacon you can as it will be the backbone to this burger's flavor.

MAKES 16

¼ lb (115 g) bacon (about 2–3 thick-cut slices)
1 lb (454 g) ground chicken
½ cup (35 g) chopped green onion
1 tsp (2 g) ground sage
½ tsp garlic powder

MIX: Roughly chop the bacon slices and put them in the food processor. Process until the bacon resembles ground meat, but not so long that the bacon becomes a paste. Add the ground chicken, green onion, sage and garlic powder to the food processor. There should be plenty of salt in the mixture already, thanks to the bacon! Pulse until the meat mixture is just combined and you can see that the green onions are evenly distributed throughout.

SHAPE: Preheat the oven to 350°F (175°C) and line a baking tray with parchment paper. Use a 2 tablespoon (30 ml) scoop to measure out 16 equal-size portions of the meat mixture and drop them onto the lined baking tray. Use your hands to roll each portion into a round mini meatball shape

BAKE: Cook the burger bites for 20 minutes and rest them for 5 minutes on the baking tray before serving. These are great paired with either BBQ Sauce (page 201) or Creamy Green Onion Dressing (page 206).

SLOW COOKER PORK SHANKS
WITH MUSHROOM GRAVY

Pork shanks...they're the short rib of the porcine world! These bone-in beauties are economically priced, full of flavor and because they're pretty lean they are perfect for the slow cooker. My favorite trick with this dish is that it makes its own gravy with just a little help from a blender.

SERVES 8

2 tsp (10 ml) coconut or avocado oil

4½ lbs (2 kg) bone-in pork shanks (see tip below)

3¼ cups (455 g) diced onion

2 cups (280 g) halved and sliced carrots (about 3 medium)

2 tsp (10 g) salt, divided

1½ lbs (680 g) white mushrooms, divided

2 cloves garlic, peeled and smashed

Juice and zest of 1 lemon

½ cup (120 ml) Pork or Chicken Broth (page 225)

2 tsp (2 g) dried oregano leaves

2 tsp (2 g) dried thyme leaves

½ tsp ground sage

COOK: Heat a large skillet over medium-high heat and add the oil. Sear the pork shanks until golden-brown, about 8 minutes per side, working in 2–3 batches. Set the pork aside in a large bowl to rest while you prep the vegetables. Add the onion, carrots and 1 teaspoon of the salt to the skillet you used to brown the pork shanks. Cook until the onion is softened, about 5 minutes. Chop 1 pound (454 g) of the mushrooms in half through the stem and add them to the skillet along with the garlic. Cook until they start to take on some color and release some of their juices into the pan, about 10 minutes. Pour the softened vegetables and the pan juices into the bottom of a 6-quart (5.5-liter) slow cooker and add the lemon juice and zest. Place the pork shanks on top of the vegetables—it's okay if you need to double-stack them on top of each other. Pour the broth over the pork shanks and cook on high for 3 hours.

BLEND: Carefully remove the pork shanks from the slow cooker and pop them into a bowl, reserving them for later. If you're making this dish for a family with small humans, take a minute to take the pork off the bones and discard them. Carefully transfer the cooking liquid and vegetables from the slow cooker to a blender. Make sure to leave a gap for the steam to escape when blending hot food—my blender has a flip-top pouring spout that I leave open. Don't fill your blender more than one-third full—work in batches if you need to, or you'll have a dangerous exploding blender! Pop a folded dish towel on top of the lid and hold the lid secure while you blend everything into a smooth gravy. Return the gravy to the slow cooker.

FINISH: Slice the remaining mushrooms in half and stir them through the gravy, along with the oregano, thyme and ground sage. Add the pork shanks back to the slow cooker and stir so that they are covered by the gravy. Cook for another hour, on high, until the mushrooms and the pork are fork tender.

TIP: The shank has two bones because it's cut from the lower leg above the hock. My butcher cuts pork shanks so that there is one bone per piece, making them look and braise just like beef short ribs. If your shanks have been cut as a cross section and have two bones, simply cut each piece in half between the two bones before browning.

SLOW COOKER RABBIT RAGÙ
WITH PORCINI MUSHROOMS

When I was growing up, my grandma would make an amazing vegetable-filled rabbit stew that was one of my favorite meals ever. Rabbit is perfect for slow cooking because it is incredibly lean—but that leanness means that it needs a little help in the flavor department. This recipe amps up the flavor by using the richness of porcini mushrooms as a foil to the shredded rabbit, while the texture is similar to a comforting chicken stew. Here I've used a slow cooker to make this meat sauce really easy to make—it's perfect over spaghetti squash or your favorite vegetable mash. This is a great recipe to keep up your sleeves for kids, too—the gravy is full of hidden vegetables. Just don't mention the bunny, okay?

SERVES 4

4 oz (120 g) bacon (about 4 slices)

3 lbs (1.4 kg) whole rabbit, cut into 6 pieces

5 cups (225 g) sliced leeks

2 cups (200 g) diced carrots

1 cup (140 g) diced onion

1 cup (120 g) diced celery

4 cloves garlic, minced

3 oz (85 g) dried porcini mushrooms

2½ cups (600 ml) Chicken Broth (page 225), divided

2 tbsp (30 ml) red wine vinegar

2 bay leaves

1 tbsp (3 g) dried rosemary leaves

2 tsp (2 g) dried thyme leaves

1 tsp (5 g) fine sea salt

BROWN: Chop the bacon into pieces and add them to a skillet over medium heat. Cook until the fat has rendered and the bacon is browned. Remove the cooked bacon with a slotted spoon and transfer it to the slow cooker. Reserve 1 tablespoon (15 ml) of the bacon fat and remove the rest from the pan—save it for cooking something else! Pat the rabbit pieces dry, then add them to the pan. Working in batches as needed, cook the rabbit in the bacon fat until you have a nice golden-brown sear on the meat, about 5 minutes per side. Reserve the browned rabbit on a plate.

COOK: Add the leeks, carrots, onion, celery and garlic to the pan and cook until softened, stirring occasionally, about 10 minutes. Transfer the softened vegetables to the slow cooker and add the dried mushrooms, too. Nestle the browned rabbit pieces on top of the vegetables and pour over any meat juices. Return the skillet to the stove and add 1 cup (240 ml) of the chicken broth. Scrape up any browned pieces from the bottom of the pan, then add that liquid to the slow cooker, along with the red wine vinegar, bay leaves, rosemary, thyme and salt. Put the lid on the slow cooker and cook on high for 3 hours.

BLEND: Carefully remove the rabbit from the slow cooker and shred the meat with two forks, discarding the bones. Add the rest of the chicken broth to the slow cooker and use an immersion blender to puree the vegetables until smooth. Add the shredded rabbit back to the slow cooker and cook until tender, about another 2 hours on high.

BEEF CHEEK STEW
WITH PEARL ONIONS

If you like beef short ribs, you will *love* beef cheeks. They are just as tender and flavorful when slow cooked, but they have much less fat and make a decadent thick, rich gravy because of their natural collagen content. And when I say tender...I mean fork tender. In fact, beef cheeks are now my favorite slow-cooking or stew meat. The other bonus point? They're usually much, much cheaper than short ribs, making them budget-friendly, to boot.

SERVES 6

3 lbs (1.4 kg) trimmed beef cheeks

1 tbsp (15 ml) coconut or avocado oil

2 cups (280 g) diced onion

4 cloves garlic, minced

3½ cups (840 ml) Beef Broth (page 224), divided

4 sprigs fresh thyme

2 bay leaves

7 oz (200 g) cauliflower florets

12 oz (340 g) frozen, peeled pearl onions

½ lb (225 g) mushrooms, sliced

½ tsp salt

BRAISE: Trim off any excess fat from the beef cheeks and cut them into 2-inch (5-cm) pieces. Heat the oil in a Dutch oven over medium-high heat on the stove top and brown the beef cheeks in batches, about 3-4 minutes per side. Reserve the browned beef cheeks on a plate to catch any juices. Preheat the oven to 325°F (163°C). Reduce the heat on the stove top to medium and add the diced onion and garlic to the Dutch oven. Cook until fragrant and just softened, about 5 minutes. Add the beef broth to the Dutch oven and scrape up the fond. Add the thyme sprigs and bay leaves, then return the browned beef cheeks to the Dutch oven and pour over any meat juices from the plate. Add the cauliflower and pop the lid onto the Dutch oven before putting it in the oven on a lower shelf. Cook for 2½ hours.

BLEND: Use a slotted spoon to transfer the beef cheeks to a bowl and keep them warm. Remove and discard the thyme sprigs and bay leaves. Use an immersion blender to puree everything into a smooth gravy.

COOK: Return the beef cheeks and any juices to the Dutch oven and add the pearl onions, sliced mushrooms and salt. Stir the beef through the gravy until all the ingredients are combined, then put the lid back on the Dutch oven and return to the oven to cook for a further 30 minutes. Serve immediately!

BACON-WRAPPED CHICKEN HEARTS

This recipe was inspired by the classic Brazilian steakhouse preparation of chicken hearts, which are skewered and quickly grilled. To add more smoky deliciousness, I've wrapped these perfectly sized bites in bacon. Soaking the chicken hearts in a brine first helps to tenderize them, so don't skip that step. Organ meats like heart are the best and most concentrated source of nutrients like vitamins, minerals, good fats and essential amino acids. This is a great way to introduce them into your diet since heart is a muscle with a texture similar to that of the regular meat of the animal it comes from. Also, this recipe has bacon. You're welcome.

SERVES 6-8

1 lb (454 g) chicken hearts
2 tbsp (30 g) kosher salt
2 cups (480 ml) filtered water
¾–1 lb (340–454 g) bacon
(see note below)

BRINE: Trim the chicken hearts, cutting off any exposed arteries and using the flat side of a knife to scrape off any excess fat. Pour the kosher salt into a freezer bag and add the water to make a quick brine and add the chicken hearts. Seal the bag and refrigerate the hearts for at least 2 hours in the brine.

WRAP: Pour off the brine and pat the hearts dry. Wrap each heart tightly with about half a strip of bacon—just enough to wrap around the heart without lots of overlap. Thread the bacon-wrapped hearts onto metal skewers or wooden skewers that have been presoaked for an hour beforehand to keep them from burning.

BROIL: Lower the oven rack to the middle of the oven—this will prevent lots of smoke from overheated bacon fat. Place the skewers on a baking sheet and broil until the bacon is crisp, about 7 minutes. Watch carefully because the bacon fat can spit or burn if it's overheated. You could also make these on an outdoor grill or on a stove-top cast-iron griddle.

NOTE: Thinly sliced bacon will crisp up better than a thick cut slice. The amount of bacon you will need will depend on the thickness of the bacon you use and the size of the chicken hearts: you will need approximately half a slice of bacon to wrap each chicken heart.

BAKED CHICKEN
WITH PEACH SAUCE

This is one of my favorite baked chicken recipes. It's got crispy skin, an easy and addictive fruity sauce and minimal ingredients. Throw in some extra light greens, like spinach, to wilt in the sauce and you've got everything you need in one pot—that's what I call winning!

SERVES 4-6

FOR THE CHICKEN

2 tsp (10 ml) coconut or avocado oil

2½ lbs (1.1 kg) bone-in, skin-on chicken thighs

1 large onion, sliced in half and then into ¼-inch (6-mm) thick crescents

1 tsp (5 g) salt

2 tsp (1 g) dried marjoram

FOR THE PEACH SAUCE

1 cup (240 ml) water

½ cup (70 g) chopped onion

½ lb (225 g) chopped peaches (about 1 large)

2 tbsp (30 ml) apple cider vinegar

2 tsp (10 ml) coconut or avocado oil

2 tsp (10 ml) coconut aminos

2 tsp (10 ml) bacon fat

1 tsp (2 g) ground ginger

¼ tsp gluten-free fish sauce

SEAR: Heat a large Dutch oven over medium-high heat and add the oil. Place the chicken thighs in the pan, skin-side down and cook until golden-brown, about 5 minutes. You may need to do this in batches, depending on the size of your Dutch oven. Rest the chicken on a plate while you prep the rest of your ingredients. Remove any excess fat from the Dutch oven, leaving about 2 teaspoons (10 ml) in the pan to soften the onions. Preheat the oven to 400°F (205°C). Reduce the heat to medium and add the onions, salt and marjoram. Toss the onions through the oil until coated and cook until softened and just beginning to brown at the edges. Remove the Dutch oven from the stove top and place on a trivet while you make the peach sauce.

BLEND: Add all the ingredients for the peach sauce to a high-power blender and blend on high until completely smooth. It will look way too thin and that's okay! It will thicken up as the chicken bakes. Pour the peach sauce into the Dutch oven and stir it through the onions. Put the seared chicken thighs on top of the sliced onions and peach sauce, keeping the browned skin out of the sauce so that it will crisp up as it cooks.

BAKE: Pop the chicken into the oven, uncovered so that the sauce will thicken as it bakes. Bake the chicken for 25–30 minutes, until the chicken is fully cooked and the sauce has thickened and reduced.

NOT CRAZY ABOUT COCONUT? Omit the coconut aminos and add an extra teaspoon (5 ml) of fish sauce.

CRISPY ORANGE VANILLA DUCK LEGS
WITH GLAZED ASIAN MUSHROOMS

Duck with crispy skin is one of my favorite things. You simply can't beat the contrast of delicious tender duck that is topped off with crispy "duck bacon," as we call it over at Meatified HQ! This is the sort of dish that looks like it's all kinds of fancy and complicated, but it's actually super simple! When I created this recipe, I couldn't decide whether to go with classic French flavors, or a little more out there with some Asian flair, so I combined the two ideas and came up with a fragrant orange and vanilla duck that's served with umami-laden mixed mushrooms that are glazed in the pan drippings. Super simple and ridiculously delicious!

SERVES 4

2 lbs (900 g) duck legs (about 4)

2 tsp (10 g) salt

3 cups (720 ml) Chicken Broth (page 225)

3 cloves garlic, minced

6 sprigs fresh thyme

1 tbsp (15 ml) vanilla extract

Juice and zest of an orange

2 bay leaves

1 cinnamon stick

1 tbsp (15 ml) balsamic vinegar

¾ lb (340 g) mixed Asian mushrooms, such as beech, oyster or enoki

BRAISE: Trim any big pieces of loose, excess skin from the duck legs, making sure to leave enough skin to cover the leg meat completely. Pat the duck legs dry and sprinkle with salt. Working in batches as needed, place the duck legs skin-side down in a hot Dutch oven on the stovetop at medium-high heat. Cook until the skin is golden brown and the fat from the skin has rendered, about 5–8 minutes. Transfer the browned duck legs to a plate. Preheat the oven to 325°F (163°C). Pour off and reserve the duck fat—keep that duck fat in the refrigerator for future cooking projects! Add the chicken broth to the Dutch oven and bring to a simmer, scraping up the fond with a spatula. Add the minced garlic, fresh thyme, vanilla extract, orange juice and zest, bay leaves and the cinnamon stick to the pan, then add the duck legs and any juices too. Cover with a lid and put the duck into the oven to braise until it is tender, about 2 hours.

CRISP: Transfer the duck to a baking dish and return the Dutch oven to the stove top. Preheat the oven to 400°F (205°C). When the oven is hot, roast the duck legs until the skin is crisp, about 15 minutes. Keep warm until ready to plate.

GLAZE: While the duck is roasting, remove and discard the thyme sprigs, bay leaves and cinnamon stick from the Dutch oven. Reserve 1 cup (240 ml) of the cooking juices and discard the rest. Bring the pan juices to a simmer over medium heat, then add the balsamic vinegar. Cook until the liquid has reduced by two thirds, then add the mushrooms. Cook until the mushrooms are tender and the liquid has reduced to a glaze, about 5 minutes. Serve the duck legs on a bed of the mixed mushrooms.

BRAISED PORK CHEEKS
WITH PUMPKIN AND SAGE

Pumpkin, sage and long slow cooking go hand in hand when it comes to the flavors and cooking methods that I turn to in the fall. In this dish, though, it's the pork cheeks that are the hero! Unlike other braising-friendly meats, pork cheeks aren't marbled with fat, and yet they still cook to fork tenderness because of the amount of connective tissue they contain, which means they're another great source of collagen and amino acids. If you've been drinking your bone broth lately, you'll know that collagen is fantastic for gut healing and something we want to incorporate into our diet as often as possible. This recipe is a great, tasty way to do that!

SERVES 6

3 lbs (1.4 kg) pork cheeks

1 tbsp (15 ml) coconut or avocado oil

2 cups (280 g) diced onion

6 cloves garlic, minced

2 cups (480 ml) Pork or Chicken Broth (page 225)

15 oz (425 ml) pumpkin puree

1 tbsp (5 g) ground sage

1 tsp (5 g) salt

10 oz (300 g) fresh spinach leaves

BROWN: Trim the pork cheeks of any large pieces of fat. Discard the fat and pat the pork cheeks dry. Heat a large Dutch oven over medium heat and add the oil. Cook the pork cheeks, working in batches as needed, until they are nicely browned, about 5 minutes per side.

BRAISE: Reserve the pork cheeks on a plate and preheat the oven to 300°F (150°C). Reduce the heat on the stove top and add the onion to the Dutch oven. Cook until softened slightly, about 5 minutes, stirring occasionally. Add the minced garlic and cook for another minute, then pour in the broth and bring to a simmer, scraping up any browned pieces from the pan with a spoon. Add the pumpkin, sage and salt, stirring to combine into a smooth sauce. Add the browned pork cheeks back to the Dutch oven and pour over any meat juices. Put on the lid and cook, covered, for 3 hours.

REDUCE: Remove the pork cheeks from the oven and add extra salt to taste, if needed—the pork cheeks should be almost fork tender at this point. Return the pork cheeks to the oven without the lid and cook, uncovered, for a further 30 minutes to reduce and thicken the sauce. Take the pork cheeks from the oven and add the spinach to the pan, stirring it through the sauce to wilt just before serving.

BEEF & BROCCOLI SLAW STIR-FRY
WITH SHIITAKE MUSHROOMS

Don't let the list of ingredients fool you. This is a simple weeknight dinner that is packed with flavor and speedy to assemble. I always keep a bag of broccoli slaw mix on hand—it's a great no-chopping-needed backup to round out a meal and here it's the backbone of this family-friendly stir-fry, standing in for typical noodles. Broccoli stalks are a great source of calcium and potassium, so being able to include them without lots of prep is a double bonus!

SERVES 4

---

1 lb (454 g) ground beef

3 cloves garlic, minced

2 tbsp (12 g) fresh minced ginger

6 green onions, chopped

¼ cup + 2 tbsp (60 ml + 30 ml) Beef Broth (page 224)

2 tbsp (30 ml) fresh orange juice

¼ cup (60 ml) coconut aminos

2 tsp (4 g) arrowroot powder

½ tsp gluten-free fish sauce

1½ tbsp (23 ml) ume plum or white wine vinegar

2 tsp (10 ml) coconut or avocado oil

12 oz (340 g) broccoli slaw mix

⅓ lb (150 g) fresh shiitake mushrooms, sliced OR 1 oz (30 g) dried shiitakes (see note)

8 oz (225 g) sliced water chestnuts, drained

BROWN: Heat a skillet over medium heat and add the ground beef. Cook the ground beef until it begins to brown, breaking up large chunks into bite-size pieces with the back of a spoon. While the ground beef is browned on the outside but still a little pink in the middle, discard any excess fat from the pan.

SIMMER: Add the garlic and ginger to the pan, cooking for a minute or so, until fragrant. Stir through the green onions, reserving the green ends for later. Add the beef broth and orange juice to the pan, then increase the heat until the liquid in the pan is bubbling gently. In a small bowl, whisk together the coconut aminos and the arrowroot powder. When the liquid in the pan has reduced by about half and the ground beef is fully cooked through, pour in the arrowroot mixture. Reduce the heat and cook until the liquid in the pan has thickened and the beef is lightly coated. Stir through the fish sauce and ume plum vinegar before removing the pan from the heat and setting aside for later.

STIR FRY: In a wok or very large high-sided skillet, add the oil over medium-high heat. When the oil is hot and shimmering, add the broccoli slaw mix, shiitake mushrooms and water chestnuts. Cook until the broccoli slaw mix begins to soften slightly, about 2 minutes. Add the seasoned beef mixture to the pan and cook until the beef is hot and the vegetables are tender. Serve immediately.

NOTE: If you're using dried shiitake mushrooms, put them in a bowl and cover them with warm water to reconstitute before you start browning the beef. When it's time to add them to the stir-fry, drain the water and pat the shiitakes dry before adding them to the pan. You can also swap the fresh shiitake mushrooms for any other mushrooms you and your family like.

NOT CRAZY ABOUT COCONUT? Omit the coconut aminos and salt. Add an extra 2 tablespoons (30 ml) of fish sauce and ½ tablespoon (8 ml) of vinegar.

SUPER SEAFOOD

I love seafood in (almost) all its forms. Nutritionally speaking, it's got all kinds of good things going on. It's high in essential vitamins and minerals and a great source of healthy omega-3 fatty acids. It's one of the most easily digestible forms of protein out there and it's insanely convenient because it's easy to find a wide variety of seafood options. You're not just limited to fresh fish, either. Frozen wild-caught seafood is a fantastic option: it's economical, readily available and thaws quickly, making it great to keep around for those "emergency" meals that crop up from time to time!

An even faster option: good quality BPA-free canned seafood like smoked oysters or sardines can do double duty as on-the-go snacks or the base of fast, and often no-cook, meals. For a super-quick lunch, try whipping up my Pan-Fried Sardines (page 104) or a speedy Smoked Seafood Spread (page 127). When it comes to weeknight meals, this chapter has you covered, with simple Poached Cod With Berry Salsa (page 119) or even a sweet Teriyaki-Glazed Salmon (page 112). If you have a little more time on the weekend, I'll even show you how to make a dairy- and coconut-free version of Fisherman's Pie (page 111)!

Exploring what the sea has to offer can be fun. Remember to aim for a variety of seafood to get the best nutritional benefits, and don't be afraid to try new things!

CRISPY SHRIMP
WITH PRESERVED LEMON AND CHIVE "MAYO"

Shrimp are almost purely protein and an awesome source of iron, which makes them a great thing to add to your diet. They're also cheap, readily available and can be thawed from frozen in minutes, so you can whip up a really quick meal if you keep them on hand. This recipe turns shrimp into lightly battered crispy nuggets with just a little arrowroot starch. Pairing them with this tangy, egg-free "mayo" means this dish has the perfect balance of protein and healthy fats.

SERVES 2-4

2 tbsp (20 g) chopped preserved lemons

½ cup (120 ml) Eggless "Mayo" (page 196)

1 tbsp (1 g) chopped fresh chives

¼ cup (30 g) arrowroot starch

1 tsp (4 g) garlic powder

½ tsp salt

1 lb (454 g) extra-large shrimp, peeled, deveined and tail-on

Coconut or avocado oil for frying

MIX: Cut the preserved lemons in half and scoop out any of the flesh: Only chop and use the preserved lemon rind. In a bowl, mix the "mayo," preserved lemon rind and chives. Stir to combine, add salt to taste, and refrigerate while you fry the shrimp.

FRY: Mix together the arrowroot starch, garlic powder and salt in a high-sided bowl. Rinse the shrimp and pat dry to remove excess moisture. Dredge the shrimp in the starch mixture to lightly coat. Pour enough oil into a skillet to almost cover the shrimp. Heat the oil to 300°F (150°C) so that it will sizzle but not spit when you add the shrimp. Working in batches, as needed (see Note below), shake the excess starch off the shrimp and fry until lightly browned, about 2 minutes per side. The cooked shrimp should look like they are coated in a lightly golden tempura batter. Transfer cooked shrimp to a paper towel-lined plate and repeat the cooking step until all the shrimp are done.

WHIP: Remove the "mayo" from the refrigerator and use a flat spatula to whip it together and soften it to a soft, smooth consistency—it will have hardened a little while chilled. Serve the crispy shrimp with the "mayo" and eat while they are piping hot!

NOTE: Use a skillet large enough that you will be able to fry the shrimp in 1–3 batches. After a few batches, the oil will begin to discolor because of the starch, which will make your crispy shrimp look over-browned. You can substitute tapioca starch for the arrowroot starch, but the finished shrimp will not be as crispy.

SALMON & AVOCADO TARTARE
WITH CRISPY "CRACKERS"

This is a nice light version of a tartare using beautiful vibrant wild-caught salmon in place of the traditional steak. This is great summer preparation, lightly dressed with plenty of fresh dill and chives, studded with creamy avocado. But the real star here is a little surprising: super-crispy salmon skin! With just a little time on the stove top, the salmon skin can be made into naturally smoky bites that can be topped and dunked into the tartare like crackers. If you ever find yourself with salmon skin that you don't need, save it in the freezer so you can make extra "crackers" for this dish—everybody always wants more and its ridiculously good for you.

SERVES 4

1 lb (454 g) skin-on, scaled salmon fillet

2 tbsp (30 ml) extra-virgin olive oil

2 tbsp (20 g) minced shallot

2 tbsp (4 g) fresh minced chives

2 tbsp (4 g) fresh minced dill

1 tsp (5 ml) gluten-free fish sauce

1 tsp (2 g) ground ginger

1 avocado

1 tsp (5 ml) coconut or avocado oil

1 lemon

MARINATE: Check the salmon for any pin bones and use tweezers to remove them if needed. Use a fillet knife to carefully slice the salmon fillet from the skin. Set the skin aside for later. Chop the salmon into a fine ¼-inch (6-mm) dice and toss together with the extra-virgin olive oil to coat. Stir through the shallot, chives, dill, fish sauce and ground ginger, then chop the avocado so that it is the same size as the diced salmon. Stir through carefully so that the avocado is evenly distributed through the mixture, but doesn't get squished. Refrigerate while you make the "crackers."

CRISP: Trim any leftover salmon still attached to the skin. Pat the skin dry—this will stop it from steaming instead of crisping. Coat a cast-iron skillet with the oil and set to medium heat. Add the salmon skin to the pan, sealed side down, and place another heavy pan or skillet on top—this will stop the salmon skin from curling at the edges. Cook for 4 minutes, until the skin is flat and beginning to crisp, then flip over and cook the other side until the skin is totally crispy, about another 2–3 minutes. Let the crisped skin cool slightly, then use a very sharp knife to cut it into 1-inch (2.5-cm) squares. Squeeze half of the lemon over the salmon tartare and stir to combine. Spoon the tartare into bowls and chop the other half of the lemon into wedges. Serve with the "crackers" and lemon wedges on the side and eat immediately!

PAN-FRIED SARDINES
WITH LIME, CILANTRO AND MINT

Sardines get a bad rap—they seem so much more intimidating compared to mild canned fish like tuna. But don't be scared! Remember, fat is flavor! While sardines might seem a little "fishier" than you're used to, they are nowhere near as strong-tasting as you might think. In fact, they're beautifully rich and "meaty" tasting and one of my favorite convenience foods these days! It's so easy to fancy up a can of good-quality fish in just a few minutes and nothing says nutrient-dense like these delicious whole little fishies. Pop open a can and top off your daily omega-3s with ease! This recipe counters the richness of the fish with plenty of lime juice and fresh herbs, making a tasty warm salad that pairs perfectly with peppery arugula.

SERVES 4

2 limes

1 tbsp (15 ml) coconut or avocado oil

4 cloves garlic, minced

4 (3.75 oz [106 g]) cans of Brisling sardines in olive oil, drained

¼ cup (10 g) fresh cilantro leaves, chopped

¼ cup (10 g) fresh mint leaves, chopped

1½ tbsp (14 g) salted capers

4 cups (100 g) arugula

½ oz (15 g) crushed pork rinds

WARM: Zest and juice the limes, reserving both the zest and the juice for later. Heat the oil in a skillet over low-medium heat. Add the garlic and cook until softened and fragrant, about a minute. Pour in the lime juice and cook until it bubbles and reduces a little, about a minute. Add the drained sardines to the pan and stir them through the oil to coat. Cook until the sardines are warmed through, another 2–3 minutes.

TOSS: Remove the pan from the heat and add the lime zest, cilantro, mint and capers, tossing to combine. Divide the arugula between plates and top the leaves with the pan-fried sardines. Sprinkle the crushed pork rinds on top and serve immediately!

BAY SCALLOP CEVICHE
WITH GRAPEFRUIT AND MINT

I love using bay scallops for ceviche because they are already perfectly bite size—and a great source of vitamin B12, to boot. They're sweeter than shrimp and fresher-tasting than the white fish often used in ceviche, as well as a great way to switch up seafood for a light lunch or appetizer. I like to pair them with grapefruit and mint for a slightly unexpected twist on classic ceviche flavors—this dish is a cilantro-free zone!

SERVES 4

1 lb (454 g) bay scallops

2 grapefruits

½ cup (70 g) diced red onion

½ tsp salt

2 tbsp (30 ml) fresh lime juice

1 tbsp (15 ml) olive oil

2 tbsp (5 g) fresh mint leaves, chopped

MARINATE: Rinse the scallops, then remove and discard any still-attached side muscles by pinching them between your thumb and finger. Drain the scallops and pat them dry. Juice one of the grapefruits. In a bowl, toss the scallops with the grapefruit juice, red onion and salt. Cover and refrigerate for 2 hours.

TOSS: Take the ceviche from the refrigerator and drain off the excess liquid. Take the remaining grapefruit and slice away the skin from the top and bottom of the fruit, making a flat surface to rest on a chopping board. Carefully cut away the rest of the grapefruit skin. Slice into the grapefruit between sections to remove just the fruit and leave behind the pith, which you can discard. Cut the grapefruit into bite-size pieces and add to the ceviche along with the lime juice and olive oil. Toss gently to combine. Season to taste with salt and add the mint leaves just before serving.

SHRIMP CAKES
WITH CILANTRO

These are my variation on traditional Thai-style fish cakes, with a little twist. Instead of the usual white fish, I've used shrimp to create a lovely crisp texture on the outside and a firm interior that reminds me of the topping on Chinese-style shrimp toasts. All of this without needing to mess around with eggs or breadcrumbs! I've kept the seasoning light and simple to let the shrimp really shine.

MAKES 8

---

1 lb (454 g) peeled and deveined shrimp

2 tbsp (5 g) fresh cilantro leaves, minced

1 tsp (4 g) garlic powder

½ tsp cream of tartar

¼ tsp baking soda

¼ tsp salt

Coconut or avocado oil for frying

MIX: Drain the shrimp in a colander, then pat them as dry as you can with a paper towel. Add the shrimp to a food processor and pulse until it has the consistency of ground meat. Add the rest of the ingredients (except the oil) to the food processor bowl and process until you have a paste. Chill for at least 15 minutes.

FRY: Divide the dough into 8 equal-size portions. Fill a skillet with 1 inch (2.5 cm) of oil and heat it to 350°F (175°C). Flatten each ball of dough so that they are about ½ inch (13 mm) thick and carefully drop the cakes into the hot oil. Cook for about 2 minutes per side, until golden-brown and crispy. The cakes will puff up a little as they cook. Eat them immediately while hot, or save them for a cold snack or lunch box addition!

FISHERMAN'S PIE
WITH PARSNIP MASH

When I was a child, this was one of my favorite things to eat—what can I say, I was a weird kid! In college, I made do with somewhat horrific frozen versions because I didn't know how to cook. I was pretty proud of myself the first time I managed to cook a from-scratch version back in the days when I still ate dairy. This version of Fisherman's Pie proves you don't need dairy to make a rich, creamy sauce and recreates my favorite comfort-food dish, filled with rich salmon, smoky mackerel and dotted with shrimp, topped off with an herbed parsnip mash. This is totally worth the wait!

SERVES 4

1 lb (454 g) parsnips

2 tbsp (30 ml) bacon fat or coconut oil

2 + ¼ cups (480 ml + 60 ml) Seafood Stock (page 225), divided

¼ tsp dried dill

2 tbsp (5 g) fresh minced flat-leaf parsley, divided

4 oz (115 g) mackerel

6 oz (170 g) skinless salmon fillet

12 oz (340 g) skinless cod fillet

10 oz (285 g) medium shrimp, peeled, deveined, tails removed

⅔ lb (300 g) cauliflower florets (about 3 cups)

1 cup (140 g) diced onion

2 cloves garlic, minced

1 bay leaf

¼ tsp ground mace

MASH: Peel the parsnips and trim off the tops. Cut the thinner ends of the parsnips into ½-inch (13-mm) pieces. Cut the thicker, tougher ends of the parsnips in half through the core first, then into ½-inch (13-mm) pieces. Add the parsnips to a saucepan and pour enough water over them to cover. Bring to a boil and then lower to a simmer, cooking until tender, about 15-20 minutes. Drain and let sit in the saucepan for a few minutes to let off steam. Add the cooked parsnips to a food processor along with the bacon fat or coconut oil and ¼ cup (60 ml) of the seafood stock; process until you have a nice mashed consistency that is as smooth or as rough as you prefer. Add the dill and 1 tablespoon (4 g) of the fresh parsley and pulse to combine. Set the mash aside for later.

POACH: Check the salmon fillet for pin bones and use tweezers to remove and discard them. Cut the cod and salmon fillet into bite-size pieces. Pour the remaining 2 cups (480 ml) of the seafood stock into a saucepan and bring to a simmer over low-medium heat. Add the cod and salmon pieces to the pan and cover with a lid. Poach until the fish is almost cooked through, about 3–4 minutes. Add the shrimp and cook until opaque, about another minute or so. Remove the pan from the heat and use a slotted spoon to transfer the cooked seafood to an 8x8-inch (20x20-cm) baking dish, making sure to reserve the cooking liquid in the pan. Flake the smoked mackerel into small pieces and sprinkle over the top of the baking dish.

BLEND: Cut the cauliflower florets into bite size pieces and add them to the saucepan with the reserved cooking liquid, diced onion, minced garlic and bay leaf. Bring the liquid to an even simmer and cook, covered, until the cauliflower is tender, about 10 minutes. Remove and discard the bay leaf. Carefully pour the cooked vegetables and cooking liquid into a blender and add the ground mace. Make sure that there is a vent for steam to escape and hold the lid of your blender with a dish towel while blending until smooth; you could also use an immersion blender to do this if you prefer. Add salt, to taste, and the rest of the fresh parsley.

BAKE: Preheat the oven to 375°F (190°C). Pour the cauliflower cream sauce over the fish, stirring through to combine. Spoon the mashed parsnips over the top of the pie filling and use a fork to spread them evenly across the dish, sealing up against the edges. Place the baking dish on a baking tray and cook until the filling is bubbling and the mash is just beginning to brown at the edges, about 40 minutes. Rest for 10 minutes before serving.

TERIYAKI-GLAZED SALMON
WITH WATERCRESS

This salmon can be on the table in well under 30 minutes, making it a perfect weeknight meal! Rich omega-3 packed salmon is paired with peppery watercress and topped with a sweet-tangy glaze and dressing that is full of flavor and simple to make. This is a great way to dress up economical frozen salmon fillets—plus the watercress has more calcium and vitamin C than spinach!

SERVES 4

FOR THE GLAZE
3 tbsp (45 ml) coconut aminos

3 tbsp (45 ml) honey

1 tbsp (15 ml) ume plum vinegar

1 tbsp (15 ml) coconut or avocado oil

1 tbsp (15 g) fresh minced ginger

1 clove of garlic, minced

½ tsp gluten-free fish sauce

1 lb (454 g) salmon, cut into 4 fillets, about 1-inch (2.5-cm) thick

4 cups (140 g) watercress

REDUCE: In a saucepan, whisk together all the ingredients for the glaze. Over a low-medium heat, bring to a simmer. Don't overheat the glaze—it will foam and bubble over if the heat is too high. Simmer gently to thicken, about 5 minutes. Remove the saucepan from the heat and reserve half of the glaze to use as a dressing later.

BROIL: Preheat the broiler on high and place the rack in the middle position. Line a baking tray with parchment paper and place the salmon fillets on top, skin-side down. Check the salmon for any pin bones and remove them. Pat the salmon dry and brush with some of the glaze from the saucepan. Broil the salmon for 3 minutes, then brush again with more glaze. Broil for another 3 minutes, then glaze again. Return the salmon to the broiler and cook until done, about another 2 minutes. The salmon is done when it is just opaque and flakes easily with a fork.

DRESS: Divide the watercress between 4 plates and top with a glazed salmon fillet. Drizzle the greens with the reserved glaze and serve!

NOT CRAZY ABOUT COCONUT? Omit the coconut aminos and add an extra 1 tablespoon (30 ml) of vinegar and an extra teaspoon (5 ml) of fish sauce.

GARLIC-ROASTED MACKEREL
WITH SALSA VERDE

When it comes to fish that are high in omega-3s, salmon tends to get all the glory. But mackerel totally deserves a chance to shine! It's full of good fats, much more economical and has a fantastically rich and buttery flavor and texture. The salsa here is full of fresh herbs, making it the perfect vibrant accompaniment for a quick, easy and light meal.

SERVES 4

¾ packed cup (30 g) fresh cilantro

¾ cup (45 g) chopped green onions

¼ cup (10 g) fresh parsley

¼ cup (60 ml) olive oil

1 tsp (3 g) salted capers

1 tbsp (15 ml) fresh lime juice

4 cloves garlic

1 tbsp (15 ml) avocado oil

8 fresh mackerel fillets, skin-on

BLEND: In a mini food processor or blender, pulse together the cilantro, green onions, parsley, olive oil, salted capers and lime juice until you get an almost-smooth salsa. Reserve the salsa for serving.

ROAST: Preheat the oven to 425°F (220°C). Line a baking tray with parchment paper. In a mortar and pestle, combine the garlic cloves and avocado oil until you have a paste—you could also mash the garlic and oil together with a fork if you don't have a mortar and pestle. Rub the fish with the garlic paste and brush the baking tray with a little oil. Lay the mackerel fillets skin-side up on the baking tray and roast until the fish flakes easily and the skin is crisp, about 10 minutes. Serve immediately with a generous spoonful of the salsa verde on each piece of mackerel.

HOT & SOUR SOUP
WITH SHRIMP "DUMPLINGS" & SEAWEED

This soup makes a great appetizer that is light but protein-packed! The distinctive pink color of cooked shrimp comes from a natural antioxidant and anti-inflammatory with an almost unpronounceable name, astaxanthin. Shrimp is also loaded up with the mineral selenium, an essential contributor to healthy thyroid function and metabolism. This soup is ridiculously delicious, with a fragrant infused broth using plenty of garlic, green onions and fresh ginger, and a nice sour kick from the tamarind paste. Seaweed is super nutritious—it's a great source of folate, vitamin B2 and manganese.

SERVES 4

FOR THE "DUMPLINGS"
1 lb (454 g) shrimp

3 garlic cloves, minced

¼ cup (10 g) cilantro leaves

2 tsp (4 g) fresh ginger, minced

2 tsp (10 ml) coconut aminos

FOR THE SOUP
8 cups (1.9 liters) Seafood Stock or Chicken Broth (page 225)

4 green onions, chopped, with the green ends reserved for garnish

4 cloves garlic, minced

1 tbsp (6 g) fresh minced ginger

¼ oz (6 g) dried mixed seaweed

2 tsp (4 g) ground ginger

2 tsp (10 ml) tamarind paste

2 tsp (10 ml) lime juice

1 tsp (5 ml) gluten-free fish sauce

MIX: Peel and devein the shrimp, then pat them dry. Add the shrimp to the bowl of a food processor and pulse until the shrimp is roughly chopped and just starting to stick together, like a meatball. Put all the remaining "dumpling" ingredients into the bowl, scrape down the sides and pulse until just combined. Line a baking tray with wax paper. Use a 1 tablespoon (15 ml) cookie scoop to drop bite-size "dumplings" onto the baking tray. Place the baking tray full of dumplings in the refrigerator for at least an hour. Don't skip this step—chilling is what will help the dumplings stay together when they are cooked in the broth later.

SIMMER: Add the stock or broth to a large saucepan. Add the green onions, garlic and minced ginger and bring the broth to a gentle simmer. Simmer for about 10 minutes to infuse the broth with flavor from the aromatics. While the broth is infusing, add the dried seaweed to a bowl and cover with cold water to reconstitute it for about 5 minutes. Add the reconstituted seaweed, ground ginger, tamarind, lime juice and fish sauce to the broth, then gently add the shrimp dumplings, too. Cook at a gentle simmer until the "dumplings" are cooked through, about 3–4 minutes.

NOT CRAZY ABOUT COCONUT? Omit the coconut aminos and add 1 teaspoon of gluten-free fish sauce to the broth.

SEARED SCALLOPS
WITH CAULIFLOWER-LEEK PUREE & ANCHOVY DRESSING

This meal looks fancy, but doesn't take long to whip together! I love scallops because they're a great source of protein and sweeter than shrimp. They can be pricy so I always wait until they go on sale to scoop them up and take home. Scallops are a great way to boost your selenium intake, which is essential for optimal thyroid health. This dish makes the most of the scallops' natural sweetness and pairs them with a creamy cauliflower-leek puree. The anchovy dressing gives a boost of extra umami and just a little bite at the end—a perfect balance of flavors.

SERVES 4

FOR THE PUREE

1 lb (454 g) cauliflower

1 medium leek, white and light-green parts only

1 clove garlic, peeled and smashed

½ cup (120 ml) Seafood Stock or Chicken Broth (page 225)

FOR THE DRESSING

6 flat anchovy fillets

¼ cup (60 ml) extra-virgin olive oil

2 tbsp (30 ml) fresh lemon juice

1 tbsp (3 g) flat-leaf parsley, chopped

1 tsp ground ginger

FOR THE SCALLOPS

1 lb (454 g) bay scallops

1 tbsp (15 ml) coconut or avocado oil, divided

Salt to taste

STEAM: Cut the cauliflower into bite-size pieces and slice the leek finely. Add the cauliflower, leek, garlic and stock or broth to a saucepan. Over medium heat, bring the broth to a simmer, then reduce the heat and cover the pan. Steam the cauliflower until just tender, about 15 minutes. Transfer the cauliflower, leek and garlic to a blender, along with any remaining cooking liquid. Leave the lid off the blender and allow the vegetables to cool slightly while you cook the scallops—this will stop the blender from exploding later when you want to make the puree!

PREP: While the cauliflower is steaming, prep your bay scallops. Pick them over and remove any still-attached side muscles by pinching them between your thumb and forefinger. Rinse the scallops and drain them in a colander, then pat them dry carefully. Any excess moisture will make the scallops steam instead of sear, so we want to get rid of it! Set the scallops aside for now while you make the dressing. Add all dressing ingredients to a mini food processor and process until the dressing is combined. Put the lid on the blender and puree the cauliflower and leeks until smooth. Season to taste with salt.

SEAR: Add the oil to a hot skillet. Once the oil is hot and shimmering (but not smoking!), sprinkle the scallops with salt on both sides and add them to the pan, making sure they don't touch each other. Cook until a crust appears on the scallops, about 4 minutes, then turn the scallops and cook for another 2–3 minutes, until both sides of the scallop are seared and the scallop is just cooked through. Divide the cauliflower-leek puree between 4 plates and top with the seared scallops. Drizzle each plate with dressing and serve immediately.

CREAMY LEEK CHOWDER
WITH SALMON

I came up with this recipe because Mr. Meatified really doesn't care for salmon very much, but I wanted him to enjoy its nutritional awesomeness. Wild-caught salmon is rich in omega-3 fatty acids, vitamin D and selenium, all of which are great for reducing inflammation in the body. You can use just 1 pound (454 g) of thawed frozen salmon and stretch it into 4 dinner-size servings of soup, which means this recipe is super economical. It's also *fast*: you can have a bowl of homemade soup on the table in about half an hour!

SERVES 4

2 tbsp (30 ml) coconut or avocado oil

4 leeks, washed, trimmed & sliced

3 cloves garlic, minced

4 cups (960 ml) of Seafood Stock or Chicken Broth (page 225)

1 tsp (1 g) dried thyme leaves

Salt to taste

¾ cup (180 ml) coconut milk

1 lb (454 g) salmon, cut into bite-size pieces

SOFTEN: Heat the oil in a large saucepan over low-medium heat. Add the chopped leeks and garlic and cook until they begin to soften but not brown, about 10 minutes.

SIMMER: Pour in the stock or broth and add the thyme leaves. Season to taste with salt and simmer about 10 minutes. Add the coconut milk to the pan. Bring back to a gentle simmer—don't boil, as the coconut milk will separate. Add the salmon and cook until it is opaque and cooked all the way through. Add salt, to taste, and ladle into bowls. Enjoy a comforting bowl of creamy soup—without a stomachache!

NOT CRAZY ABOUT COCONUT MILK? Omit the coconut milk. Add 1 cup (240 g) of diced white sweet potato or cauliflower florets to the soup and cook until tender. Puree everything together in the pan with an immersion blender before adding the salmon.

POACHED COD
WITH BERRY SALSA

Like many people, growing up my only real encounter with white fish of any kind was...battered and fried. Without that gluten bomb of a coating, white fish seemed pretty bland to me. Then I realized the power of a punchy salsa! The firm meaty texture of the fish is a great contrast to the simple summery berry salsa and is one of my favorite dishes now. You don't have to stick to cod for this one—any firm white fish will work here, like hake or haddock.

SERVES 4

FOR THE SALSA

1 cup (150 g) chopped strawberries

½ cup (70 g) blueberries

½ cup (70 g) diced red onion

¼ cup (10 g) cilantro, chopped

2 tbsp (30 ml) olive oil

Zest and juice of one lime

Pinch salt

FOR THE FISH

1 tbsp (15 ml) coconut or avocado oil

2 smashed garlic cloves

½ cup (120 ml) Seafood Stock (page 225) or clam juice

2 tbsp (30 ml) lemon juice

Salt to taste

1 lb (454 g) cod, cut into 4 [1-inch (2.5-cm)] thick fillets

SMASH: Add all the salsa ingredients to a food processor and pulse until just combined, leaving chunks of fruit still visible in the salsa. Set aside to top the fish with later.

POACH: Add the oil to a skillet over low-medium heat. When the oil is hot, add the smashed garlic cloves and cook until fragrant. Add the seafood stock or clam juice and lemon juice and then bring the liquid to a simmer, adding salt to taste. Simmer for about 5 minutes to reduce slightly, then reduce the heat so that the poaching liquid is barely simmering and add the cod fillets to the pan. Cover the pan and cook until the fish is opaque and flakes easily, about 6–8 minutes. Serve the cod topped with the berry salsa—it is a great warm dish when freshly made, but also makes a great leftovers lunch when cold, especially with some added salad greens!

SHUCKED OYSTERS
WITH STRAWBERRY "MIGNONETTE"

This is a hot sauce–free zone! I've always liked to keep seafood simple, especially when it comes to something as delicate as oysters. Here I've replaced the usual not-so-gut-friendly hot sauce with a delicious, tangy and fresh topping—you may never want to eat oysters another way after this, according to Mr. Meatified! And when it comes to nutrient density, these bad boys are the bomb. Load up your plates with deliciousness and get a mega dose of zinc, iron, calcium and vitamin B12!

MAKES 2 DOZEN OYSTERS

½ cup (120 ml) white wine vinegar

1 shallot, minced finely

24 fresh oysters

2 tbsp (10 g) finely diced strawberries (about 4)

2 tbsp (4 g) finely chopped fresh chives

MARINATE: Mix together the white wine vinegar and minced shallot in a bowl. Soaking the shallot in the vinegar will help mellow out the shallot flavor—set the "mignonette" base aside while you shuck your oysters.

SHUCK: Fill a large bowl or platter with crushed ice. Carefully pop the oysters open with an oyster knife, keeping the oyster level at all times so as not to lose any of the natural juice. Work the oyster knife into the hinge of the oyster and turn the knife at a 45 degree angle to work open the oyster. When it pops, slide the oyster knife around the side of the oyster until both halves of the shell are separated. Carefully use the oyster knife to detach the oyster from the shell. Remove and discard the top flat side of the shell and carefully wipe any grit or sand from the edges of the shell with a cloth. Repeat for each oyster. Place each oyster half on the crushed ice and nestle the shells in so that they stay level and retain all that delicious briny liquid in the shells.

DRIZZLE: Add the diced strawberries to the vinegar mixture and spoon a little over each oyster. Sprinkle the chopped chives over the oysters and serve immediately!

NOTE: If you like to pair your oysters with horseradish, use one of the recipes for Horseradish Two Ways (page 218).

STEAMED MUSSELS
WITH GARLIC POTATO PUREE

This is a super-simple dish to make, but looks so elegant that people will never believe how little time it takes to whip up! Don't panic about the amount of garlic: it mellows out beautifully and helps make a lovely creamy puree without needing to use any coconut milk.

SERVES 4

1 tbsp (15 ml) coconut or avocado oil

1 head of garlic, peeled and minced

1 shallot, finely sliced

¼ cup (30 g) celery, finely chopped

½ tsp (4 g) salt

2 tsp (3 g) fresh rosemary, chopped

2 + ¼ cups (480 ml + 60 ml) Seafood Stock (page 225), divided

1 cup (240 ml) water

2 bay leaves

¼ lb (114 g) peeled, diced white sweet potato

1 tsp lemon juice

3 lbs (1.4 kg) fresh mussels

SIMMER: Add the oil to a saucepan over low heat. Add the garlic, shallot, celery and salt and cook until softened and fragrant, but not browned, about 10 minutes. Add the rosemary and cook until fragrant, about a minute. Add 2 cups (480 ml) of the seafood stock, water, bay leaves and white sweet potato. Turn up the heat to a simmer and cook until the sweet potato is soft, about 10 minutes. Remove and discard the bay leaves, then stir in the lemon juice. Use an immersion blender to puree everything together until smooth and keep warm.

CLEAN: Scrub the mussels under cold running water to get rid of any grit or sediment. Pull off the "beard" from each one by pulling it toward the wide end of the shells. Discard any mussels that are already opened if they don't close when you tap on their shell.

STEAM: Add the remaining ¼ cup (60 ml) of seafood stock to a large skillet and heat on high. Add the mussels, cover with a lid and steam until the shells have opened and the mussels are cooked through, about 5 minutes. Discard any unopened mussels. Divide the puree between bowls and top with the steamed mussels—you won't be able to get this dish to the table fast enough!

CRAB SOUP
WITH RADISHES

I adore crab, but it's often super expensive. This soup is one of the recipes I use to make crab go a little further and make the most of its delicate sweetness by keeping the soup light and fragrant with ginger and shallots. I finish the soup with some sliced radishes to give just a hint of heat. This soup is delicious, soothing and a recipe that I turn to again and again!

SERVES 4

2 tsp (10 ml) coconut or avocado oil

2 tbsp (12 g) fresh minced ginger

4 cloves garlic, minced

2 shallots, minced

3 cups (720 ml) Chicken Broth (page 225)

2 cups (480 ml) Seafood Stock (page 225) or clam juice

3 oz (85 g) radishes

1 tsp (5 ml) gluten-free fish sauce

2 tbsp (30 ml) fresh lime juice

½ lb (225 g) lump crab meat

4 green onions, chopped, green tops only

SIMMER: Add the oil to a saucepan over low heat. Toss the ginger, garlic and shallots in the oil and cook until softened, about 5 minutes. Add the chicken broth and seafood stock or clam juice. Turn up the heat and bring just to a boil, then reduce the heat to a simmer, cooking for another 10 minutes or so. While the broth is simmering, use a mandoline to chop the radishes into ⅛-inch (3-mm) slices and set aside for later. Add the fish sauce, lime juice and crab meat, cooking until the crab is warmed through. Stir the sliced radishes through the broth and remove the pan from the heat. To serve, divide the soup between bowls and garnish with the chopped green onions.

PROSCIUTTO-WRAPPED TROUT ROLLS
WITH ZUCCHINI-LEEK STUFFING

This is one of those recipes that looks *waaaay* fancier than it is. Thin fillets of fish like trout are perfect for stuffing and baking because they cook evenly and quickly without drying out. Here I've used my Zucchini-Leek Spread (page 215) as a no-bread-crumbs-needed stuffing that is light and packed with flavor. Wrapping the rolled stuffed fillets with prosciutto adds a lovely extra dimension of flavor and ensures that the rolls don't unroll!

SERVES 4

4 slices of prosciutto
4 (5-oz [150-g]) skinless trout fillets
1 cup of Zucchini-Leek Spread (page 215)

ROLL: Preheat the oven to 350°F (175°C). Lay the prosciutto slices out flat on a chopping board. Lay the trout fillets on top of the prosciutto slices, lining the thinnest end of the trout flush with the edge of the prosciutto. If you want to get fancy and make your rolls super pretty, trim the trout fillets so they are the same width as the prosciutto slices. Don't worry if you don't bother with trimming, it's just for looks! Spoon a quarter of the Zucchini-Leek Spread onto each piece of fish and press it evenly across the fillets, leaving about an inch (2.5 cm) of the fillet without stuffing at the thinnest ends—this will stop the stuffing from spilling out at the bottom of the rolls. Starting from the thickest end of the fillets, tightly roll the prosciutto and trout in on themselves, forming a stuffed trout spiral that is wrapped in prosciutto.

BAKE: Place the rolls in a baking tray or dish lined with parchment paper, with the ends of the fillets on the bottom. Press down lightly to seal the rolls and bake until the fish is fully cooked through and opaque, about 15–18 minutes. For pretty presentation, slice each roll in half widthwise to make two spirals per serving—or to split for a lighter lunch. I like to serve this on a bed of arugula, drizzled with a little olive oil and lemon juice.

SWITCH IT UP: Don't have any Zucchini-Leek Spread? Try using your favorite AIP-friendly pesto, instead! Any other thin fillet of fish would work instead of trout for this recipe—try making it with Dover sole!

SMOKED SEAFOOD SPREAD
WITH SARDINES AND OYSTERS

This is one of the easiest and tastiest ways to get a great dose of omega-3 fats, by using a mixture of already cooked sardines and oysters. The smokiness of the seafood is balanced with lemon and parsley and the resulting pâté is deceptively rich and decadent.

MAKES 8 OZ (225 G)

1 (3.75 oz [106 g]) can of smoked sardines in extra-virgin olive oil

1 (3.75 oz [106 g]) can of smoked oysters in extra-virgin olive oil

2 tbsp (30 ml) coconut milk

2 tbsp (5 g) fresh parsley

1 tbsp (15 ml) lemon juice

2 green onions, chopped, white parts only

MASH: Drain the can of sardines, reserving 1 tablespoon (15 ml) of the olive oil. Put half of the sardines in a bowl and mash them roughly with a fork. Set aside for now.

PROCESS: Add the remaining sardines to a mini food processor. Drain the oysters and add them to the food processor bowl. Pour in the reserved olive oil, the coconut milk, parsley, lemon juice and green onions. Process until almost smooth, with flecks of green onion and parsley dotted through the mixture. Add the mashed sardines and pulse until just combined—this gives the spread a nice texture, but you could also puree the spread until completely smooth, if you wished.

CHILL: Pour the spread into a bowl or ramekin and cover tightly. Chill for at least 2 hours. Will keep for several days if refrigerated. Use as a spread on cucumber slices, as part of a salad or as a topping for hot roasted sweet potatoes.

NOT CRAZY ABOUT COCONUT? Omit the coconut milk and add an extra 1-2 tablesoons (15-30 ml) of olive oil from the can.

QUICK PICKLED SHRIMP
WITH RADISHES

Flavor-wise, this dish is like a cross between a classic citrus-laced ceviche and a vinegar-based cocktail sauce since the shrimp are pickled in a mixture of lemon juice and apple cider vinegar. The result is a delightfully crispy shrimp, flavored with lemon, garlic and dill, and tossed with radishes for extra crunch. Quick Pickled Shrimp can last for a week or so in the fridge, which means I usually make a batch to keep for quick emergency protein snacks or to toss over some greens for a speedy salad lunch.

SERVES 4

1 lb (454 g) peeled and deveined large shrimp

½ cup (120 ml) apple cider vinegar

¼ cup (60 ml) lemon juice

2 tbsp (30 ml) extra-virgin olive oil

3 cloves garlic, minced

2 tbsp (4 g) fresh chopped dill

¼ tsp salt

Zest of one lemon

4 thinly sliced radishes

¼ cup (35 g) thinly sliced red onion

BLANCH: On the stovetop, bring a pot of salted water to a boil. Drop the shrimp into the boiling water and cook until opaque and fully cooked through, about a minute or two. Drain the shrimp and put them under cold running water to cool them down and to stop them from cooking further. When the shrimp are cool to the touch, let them drain again.

PICKLE: In a bowl, mix together the apple cider vinegar, lemon juice, olive oil, garlic, dill, salt and lemon zest. Add the cooked and cooled shrimp and toss to combine so that the shrimp are coated in the liquid. Let the shrimp sit in the vinegar mixture for 20 minutes. Use a mandolin to thinly slice the radishes and onion to about ⅛-inch (3-mm) thick, then toss them with the shrimp. You can serve the shrimp immediately at this point—or you can refrigerate in jars for up to a week. The longer the shrimp are pickled, the pinker the pickling liquid will become.

ANCHOVY-STUFFED PORTOBELLOS
WITH PANCETTA

Don't worry, I'm not talking those super-salty, "mostly good for dressing" anchovies! This recipe uses canned whole anchovy fillets that are packaged in olive oil—just like sardines. In fact, if you can't find anchovies, you can sub sardines in their place here. Both of those options will give you a meal that is packed with healthy omega-3 fatty acids. We like those. These kinds of healthy canned fish are a great pantry staple to keep on hand. This recipe uses these underrated little fish as a rich stuffing for mushrooms, paired with the saltiness of pancetta and a little zing from fresh parsley and lemon. Don't be weirded out by the avocado; it adds a lovely creaminess that holds all the other flavors—and the stuffing—together.

SERVES 4

4 portobello mushrooms

4 oz (115 g) pancetta

3 cloves garlic, minced

1 cup (140 g) onion, diced

2 (4.37 oz [124 g]) cans anchovy or sardine fillets in olive oil, drained

½ cup (120 g) mashed avocado (about 1 small)

2 tbsp (5 g) fresh minced parsley

2 tsp (10 ml) lemon juice

1 tsp (1 g) dried oregano leaves

PREP: Preheat the oven to 400°F (205°C). Use a spoon to scrape out the gills from the middle of the mushrooms, but leave them intact near the edges or the caps will flatten and collapse when they're cooked. Mince the mushroom stems and gills finely. In a small skillet over low-medium heat, cook the pancetta until the fat renders and it begins to brown. Remove the pancetta from the skillet with a slotted spoon and add it to bowl. Add the garlic, diced onion and reserved mushroom stems and gills to the skillet. Cook them in the leftover pancetta fat until the onions soften, about 5 minutes, then add them to the bowl with the pancetta. Line a baking tray with parchment paper and place the mushrooms on the tray, caps down. Roast for 10 minutes, then remove the roasted mushrooms from the oven.

STUFF: While the mushrooms are roasting, add the anchovy or sardines, as well as the avocado to the bowl with the rest of the stuffing ingredients. Use a fork to mash them together gently, then fold in the minced parsley, lemon juice and oregano leaves to finish the stuffing mixture. When the mushrooms are removed from the oven, use tongs to flip them over and drain out the excess moisture in the caps. Place them back on the baking tray and pat the inside of each cap with a paper towel to make sure they're dry. Divide the stuffing mixture evenly between the caps, then return the stuffed portobellos to the oven and bake until the filling is piping hot, about 10 minutes. That's it!

SNEAKY TUNA SALAD
WITH GREEN ONION DRESSING

What makes this a "sneaky" tuna salad? Mr. Meatified claims he doesn't like sardines and refuses to eat them. But, uh…I'm afraid he often just doesn't *know* he's eating them. Because I hide them. In places like this tuna salad. Why would I do such a tricky thing? Well, tuna is a great source of protein, it's true. But if we're talking good quality fats, sardines are where it's at. The ugly-but-tasty sardine is full of omega-3s—about one and a half times those in tuna—and you all know how awesome I think they are! The other bonus to this salad? It's possible to get great quality wild-caught tuna *and* sardines for a decent price, plus you can stash a can or two in the pantry for emergency hungry times!

SERVES 4

2 (5 oz [142 g]) cans of wild caught tuna

2 (3.75 oz [106 g]) can of wild-caught sardines

1 batch of Creamy Green Onion Dressing (page 206)

½ cup (60 g) cucumber, peeled and chopped into bite-size pieces

½ cup (75 g) olives in olive oil, drained

¼ cup (35 g) red onion, diced

6 oz (170 g) mixed salad greens

MIX: In a bowl, break up the tuna and sardines with a fork to combine. Pour in the Creamy Green Onion Dressing and add the cucumber, olives and red onion. Combine with a fork.

ASSEMBLE: Divide the mixed greens between plates. Top with the Sneaky Tuna Salad and serve.

SALT-CURED SALMON
WITH ORANGE & DILL

I love salmon, not just because of its rich flavor but also because it's such a great source of healthy fats. I love cured salmon even more...but the price? Not so much! So what do I do instead of spending a small fortune on teeny tiny packages of my favorite cured fish? Wait until there's a sale on wild-caught fresh salmon—and then make my own! I especially love making cured salmon with plenty of dill and a lot of citrus zest—it adds extra fresh flavors and is a fantastic compliment to the richness of the fish.

MAKES ABOUT 14 OZ (395 G)

1½ lbs (680 g) skin-on salmon fillet, 1-inch (2.5-cm) thick

⅓ cup (30 g) kosher salt

Zest of 3 oranges

¼ cup (8 g) fresh dill, chopped, tough stems discarded

CRUST: Cut the salmon fillet into two equally-sized pieces and check it for any remaining pin bones. If you find any, pull them out carefully with some kitchen tweezers. Mix together the kosher salt, orange zest and dill so that it looks like a colorful sand. Lay out a piece of foil large enough to wrap the salmon in, then place a piece of parchment paper of the same size on top of the foil. Place the two salmon fillets on top of the parchment paper, skin-side down, and divide the salt mixture evenly between them. Make sure each fillet is evenly coated with the salt mixture, pressing it gently into the fish. Place one of the fillets on top of the other, so that the skin side is facing upward on the top piece and both salt-coated sides of the fish are pressed against each other. Wrap the salmon up tightly in the parchment paper and foil, then place in a high-sided dish.

CURE: Place another dish on top of the salmon to help weigh it down and further press the salt cure into the salmon. Refrigerate while it cures, anywhere from 12 hours—2 days, depending on how firm (or how salty) you like your salmon. When the salmon is cured to your taste, rinse off the salt mixture under cold running water, then pat dry. Put the cured salmon pieces into a clean dish or baking tray and refrigerate, uncovered, for another 24 hours.

SLICE: Once the salmon has air dried, it is ready for slicing! Use a sharp knife to thinly slice the salmon at an angle straight off the skin. The cured salmon can be eaten immediately, or wrapped up tightly and eaten within a week or so.

4

EAT THE RAINBOW

Just as it's important to eat a variety of different proteins for optimal nutrition and healing, it's the same when it comes to produce. Eating a variety of vegetables and fruits is going to give you the best array of vitamins and minerals and their health benefits. Vegetables, especially, are packed with all the antioxidants, vitamins, minerals and fiber that will help promote a healthy gut and promote healing from the inside out.

One of the best ways to ensure you are eating that kind of variety is to think in terms of colors. Eating across the different colors from purple to red to orange to yellow to green (and more) will give you the best nutritional head start in the kitchen and beyond, since each of the different colors are indicative of specific nutrients, like carotenoids (in orange/red vegetables), chlorophyll (in greens) or antioxidants like anthocyanins (found in purple vegetables). Eating the rainbow is one way to look at things, but don't forget that you need to mix up your choices even within color groups. For example, swap out spinach for watercress and you're getting lots more vitamin K…but you're losing out on calcium. So eating as many different types of vegetables and fruits as possible is the best way to ensure that you are getting the widest nutritional spectrum.

It can be easy to fall into a produce rut, eating the same things cooked or prepared in the same ways. This chapter is all about avoiding that rut and gives you an array of salads, soups and sides that will make it easy to "eat the rainbow." I've taken familiar preparations and given them a little flavor twist, like with my Roasted Asparagus With Double Apple Dressing (page 148) or Caramelized Brussels Sprouts With Lime & Crispy Shallots (page 140). I've recreated familiar non-AIP-friendly recipes in ways that make them nutritious and gut-healing, like my Collard Greens with Parsnip "Cream" (page 145) or the Green Papaya Salad With Shrimp & Radishes (page 139). I really want you to take away from this chapter that side dishes can be fun and vegetables can even become the star of the show!

PARSNIP WEDGES
WITH GARLIC "MAYO" DIPPING SAUCE

Move over potatoes, parsnip wedges are here! Fluffy in the middle with crispy edges, these wedges have a touch of sweetness that pairs perfectly with a garlicky dipping sauce. The only problem? These will disappear so fast, you should probably make a double batch.

SERVES 4

FOR THE DIPPING SAUCE
1 tsp (5 ml) coconut or avocado oil

3 cloves garlic, minced

½ cup (120 ml) Eggless "Mayo" (page 196)

FOR THE PARSNIP WEDGES
1 lb (454 g) parsnips

1 tbsp (15 ml) coconut or avocado oil

1 tbsp (15 ml) lime juice

1 tsp (5 g) salt

½ tsp garlic powder

BLEND: Add the oil and minced garlic to a pan over low heat and cook until softened and fragrant, about a minute or so. Let the garlic cool and then stir or blend it into the "mayo." Set the sauce aside for now.

BOIL: Peel the parsnips, then trim and discard the ends. Cut each parsnip in half widthwise so that you have one thicker and one thinner piece from each parsnip. Cut the parsnips into wedges: slice the thicker pieces in half lengthways and then cut each half into quarters so that you have 8 wedges. Slice the thinner pieces lengthwise into 2-4 wedges. Cover the parsnips with water and bring the pan to a boil. Reduce the heat to a simmer and cook until only just tender, about 8–10 minutes. You want to be able to pierce the parsnips with a fork without them breaking into pieces, so don't overcook them!

ROAST: Preheat the oven to 425°F (220°C). Drain the parsnips and tip them out onto a clean dish towel. Spread them out in a single layer and let the steam evaporate for a few minutes. Mix together the oil, lime juice, salt and garlic powder in a large bowl. When the parsnips are dry on the outside, add them to the bowl and toss carefully to coat in the flavored oil. Place an oven-safe metal baking rack onto a baking tray. Lay the parsnip wedges out on the rack, spacing them out so that they don't touch. Roast the parsnip wedges for 15 minutes. Turn the parsnips over and return them to the oven for another 10–15 minutes, until both sides are browned. Serve the wedges immediately, with the "mayo" for dipping.

GREEN PAPAYA SALAD
WITH SHRIMP & RADISHES

There's nothing more satisfying when it comes to food textures than crunchy. At least if you're me. Maybe I was a cartoon bunny in a former life. But carrots get old, so this is one of my new favorite crunchy healthy foods: green papaya. Green papayas make a light and refreshing salad and soak up all the flavor from this tangy-sour dressing. Pairing the salad with some simple shrimp packs in some extra protein and proves that salad can be a meal!

SERVES 4

3 cloves garlic

3 tbsp (18 g) dried shrimp

¼ cup + 2 tbsp (90 ml) lime juice

3 tbsp (45 ml) coconut aminos

2 tbsp (30 ml) avocado oil or
light-tasting olive oil

1½ tbsp (23 ml) gluten-free fish sauce

6 cups (540 g) green papaya, peeled,
seeded and shredded or julienned

1 lb (454 g) shrimp, cleaned and
deveined

2 green onions, chopped

3 tbsp (8 g) fresh cilantro leaves,
chopped

3 tbsp (6 g) fresh mint leaves, chopped

6 radishes, sliced finely

DRESS: Add the garlic and dried shrimp to a mini food processor and process until very finely chopped. Add the lime juice, coconut aminos, oil and fish sauce and pulse to combine. Put the shredded green papaya in a large bowl and pour the dressing over it. Toss to coat and set aside while you cook the shrimp.

BLANCH: Place a large bowlful of iced water in the sink. Bring a pot of salted water to a boil. Cook the shrimp until just opaque and cooked through, about 2–4 minutes, depending on the size of the shrimp. Drain the shrimp and plunge into the ice water to cool. Once the shrimp are cool, drain and pat dry.

TOSS: Add the cooled and dried shrimp to the salad and toss with the salad dressing. To serve, divide the salad between bowls and garnish with the chopped green onions, cilantro, mint and radishes. Slurping is encouraged!

NOT CRAZY ABOUT COCONUT? Omit the coconut aminos and add 2 tablespoons (30 ml) of chicken broth, as well as an additional tablespoon (15 ml) of fish sauce.

CARAMELIZED BRUSSELS SPROUTS
WITH LIME & CRISPY SHALLOTS

Mr. Meatified still says he hates brussels sprouts. But he loves them when they're cooked like this. Slicing the brussels sprouts super finely makes them caramelize all over instead of just on the outside and the lime juice creates a tangy glaze. Topping them off with crispy shallots makes these "mini cabbages" crispy-crunchy and downright addictive! Brussels are packed with vitamin K and vitamin C, to boot, making them a badass vegetable when it comes to potent anti-inflammatory benefits!

SERVES 4

2 shallots

2 tbsp (30 ml) coconut or avocado oil, divided

1 lb (454 g) brussels sprouts

½ tsp salt

¼ cup (60 ml) fresh lime juice (about 2 limes)

CRISP: Peel the shallots and cut each in half. Slice the shallots finely. In a large skillet over low-medium heat, add 1 tablespoon (15 ml) of oil. When the oil is hot and beginning to shimmer, add the shallots and toss them in the oil to coat, then spread them out in a single layer. Cook until golden, stirring frequently to avoid burning, about 5–8 minutes. Once the shallots are golden-brown and crispy, remove them from the oil with a slotted spoon and transfer them to a paper towel–lined plate to cool. Watch them carefully as the shallots will burn easily—it's better to take them out when they still look a little underdone, especially if you're cooking them in a black skillet!

CARAMELIZE: Cut the stems from the bottom of each sprout and discard. Pull off any loose leaves and slice the rest of the sprouts finely. Add the remaining oil to the skillet and increase the heat to medium-high. Add the loose leaves and the sliced brussels sprouts to the pan, along with the salt. Cook until the brussels sprouts begin to caramelize at the edges, about 5 minutes. Add the lime juice and toss to coat. Continue to cook until caramelized and just tender, about 8 minutes. Top with the reserved crispy shallots and either serve immediately as a side, or let cool slightly and use as a salad base.

SWEET POTATO GRATIN
WITH CARAMELIZED ONIONS

You don't need dairy to make an insanely decadent gratin dish—pinky promise! This is the perfect comforting fall or winter dish: layers of sweet potato in a velvety sauce, heightened by the richness of caramelized onions. You can't go wrong with this and most people don't even notice that it's dairy-deficient.

SERVES 6

1½ tbsp (23 g) coconut butter

1½ tbsp (15 g) coconut flour

13.5 oz (400 ml) coconut milk

¾ cup (180 ml) pumpkin puree

⅓ cup (80 ml) Chicken Broth (page 225)

1 tsp (4 g) garlic powder

½ tsp dried thyme leaves

½ tsp salt

1½ lbs (680 g) sweet potatoes

½ cup (115 g) Speedy Caramelized Onions (page 210)

SAUCE: In a saucepan over low heat, gently melt the coconut butter until it's liquid. Warm it through, but don't let it get hot enough to toast or brown. Sift the coconut flour and add it to the pan, stirring to combine it with the coconut butter—it will look a little like crumbs and works in place of a roux to thicken the sauce. Slowly add the coconut milk a little at a time, stirring to combine the mixture smoothly each time—this way you'll avoid making a lumpy sauce! Warm the coconut milk mixture through, then add the pumpkin puree and chicken broth. Stir to combine until smooth, then add the garlic, thyme and salt. Remove the pan from the heat and reserve the sauce for later.

LAYER: Preheat the oven to 400°F (205°C). Use a mandoline to slice the sweet potatoes ⅛-inch (3-mm) thick. Pour some of the sauce mixture into an 8x8-inch (20x20-cm) baking dish—enough to just cover the bottom of the pan. Arrange a layer of overlapping sweet potato slices in the bottom of the dish, pressing them down into the sauce gently. Top the sweet potato slices with one-third of the caramelized onions and spoon over a little of the sauce. Repeat until all the sweet potato and caramelized onion have been used up—you should have about 4 layers of sweet potato. Pour over the remaining sauce mixture, using a spatula to level it off and make sure that all the sweet potato is covered. Bake until the sweet potato is tender, about 45–50 minutes. Rest the gratin for 10 minutes before slicing and serving.

HERBED SPAGHETTI SQUASH
WITH BACON AND "BREAD CRUMBS"

This is one of my go-to weeknight sides as it takes just minutes to whip up if I've pre-roasted a spaghetti squash over the weekend! You can't go wrong with garlic and bacon...but the best part of this dish is the crispy topping. Instead of traditional bread crumbs, crushed pork rinds are the secret weapon here and contrast perfectly with the squash.

SERVES 4

1 medium spaghetti squash,
 about 3 lbs (1.4 kg)

4 slices bacon

4 cloves garlic, minced

2 tbsp (30 ml) fresh lemon juice

⅓ oz (9 g) pork rinds

2 tbsp (8 g) nutritional yeast

¼ cup (10 g) fresh basil, chopped

ROAST: Preheat the oven to 400°F (205°C). Line a baking tray with parchment paper. Use a knife to carefully poke holes evenly across the spaghetti squash skin, then place on the baking tray and roast until the squash is tender, about 45 minutes to 1 hour. Remove from the oven and let cool for 15 minutes. Transfer the squash to a chopping board and carefully cut it in half, taking care to avoid any steam. Scoop out the seeds and discard. Use a fork to scrape the squash threads into "spaghetti" like strands.

SEASON: Cook the bacon in a skillet over medium heat, until crisp. Set the bacon aside to cool. Leave 2 tablespoon (30 ml) of the bacon fat in the pan—pour off any excess and reserve it for future use. Reduce the heat and add the minced garlic to the pan, cooking until it softens but doesn't brown, about 1 minute. Add the spaghetti squash strands to the pan and toss through the garlic oil, coating in the bacon fat. Cook until the squash is warmed through, about 3 minutes. Squeeze over the lemon juice and cook for a minute or so, until the liquid is absorbed. Remove the skillet from the heat.

TOP: Add the pork rinds and nutritional yeast to a mini food processor and pulse into bread crumb–size pieces. Stir the fresh basil through the spaghetti squash and top with the "bread crumbs" just before serving.

COLLARD GREENS
WITH PARSNIP "CREAM"

Everybody knows that they're supposed to eat their greens. There's a great reason for that—they are a fantastic source of calcium. One of my favorite ways to eat greens used to be creamed...with plenty of dairy products. But guess what? You don't need dairy here at all. This recipe packs a vegetable double whammy as the slight bitterness of collard greens is balanced out by the mellow sweetness of the parsnip "cream." This dish has all the silkiness of a creamed greens recipe and is a great make ahead dish. You can gently reheat it and it will last a few days in the refrigerator, too. Now there's no excuse not to get your greens on!

SERVES 4

FOR THE GREENS

¾ cup (180 ml) Chicken Broth (page 225)

½ tsp salt

1 lb (454 g) collard greens, sliced in ½-inch (13-mm) thick ribbons

FOR THE "CREAM"

2 tsp (10 ml) bacon fat

¾ cup (105 g) onion, diced

2 cloves garlic, peeled

½ lb (225 g) parsnips, peeled and sliced

1 cup (240 ml) Chicken Broth (page 225), divided

WILT: Add the chicken broth and salt to a large, high-sided pan over medium-high heat. Add half of the collard greens to the pan and cook until they wilt, about 3 minutes. Add the rest of the collard greens and cook until they are also wilted down. Lower the heat to medium and cover the pan, leaving a small gap for steam to escape if the lid does not have a vent. Cook, stirring every 5 minutes or so, until the collard greens are just tender, about 15–20 minutes. Remove from the heat. If there is any leftover cooking liquid, discard it.

PUREE: While the collard greens are cooking, heat a large skillet with the bacon fat on medium-low. Add the onion and cook until it is just beginning to caramelize at the edges, about 10 minutes. Add the garlic cloves, parsnips and ½ cup (120 ml) of the chicken broth. Cover the pan and bring to a simmer, cooking until the parsnips are tender, about 10–15 minutes. Remove the pan from the heat. Pour the parsnip mixture carefully into a high-power blender. Add the remaining chicken broth and blend on high, scraping down the sides once or twice to make sure you get a smooth "cream." Add salt, to taste.

WARM: Pour the parsnip "cream" over the cooked collard greens and stir through. Return to the stove top and warm through gently before serving.

NOTE: You can use this "cream" sauce for lots of other vegetables if you want to—this recipe will make just over 1 cup (240 ml) of sauce.

ORANGE SALAD
WITH OLIVE ROSEMARY TAPENADE

Olives are often reviled because of their fat content, but they're actually a source of healthy saturated fats. Traditionally, tapenade is more like a spreadable paste, but this version is a little more of a coarse finish so that I could almost scatter it over fresh orange slices for a lovely contrast of savory and sweet flavors.

SERVES 4

4 large oranges

2 tbsp (10 g) orange zest

1½ cups (215 g) pitted green olives in olive oil, drained

3 cloves garlic, peeled

2 tbsp (30 ml) lemon juice

2 tbsp (5 g) fresh flat-leaf parsley

2 tsp (3 g) fresh rosemary, chopped

¼ cup + 2 tbsp (90 ml) extra-virgin olive oil

½ red onion, thinly sliced

SLICE: Zest 2 of the oranges to get the 2 tablespoons (10 g) of orange zest for the tapenade. Set aside for later. Use a serrated knife to remove the rest of the skin and pith. Slice each orange into 5–6 slices and set aside.

BLITZ: Add the orange zest, olives, garlic, lemon juice, parsley and rosemary to the bowl of a food processor. Pulse until everything begins to combine but is still chunky. Scrape down the sides of the bowl and slowly add the olive oil until the tapenade is combined.

ASSEMBLE: Layer the orange slices onto plates and top with the red onion slices. Spoon over the olive rosemary tapenade. Drizzle with a little more extra-virgin olive oil, if you wish.

ROASTED ASPARAGUS
WITH DOUBLE APPLE DRESSING

I love asparagus in pretty much any form. But my absolute favorite way to cook asparagus is—hands down—roasting. It brings out all the natural flavor, while adding a little extra dimension with a few tasty crispy spots. Drizzling the just-roasted asparagus with something acidic once it's roasted amps that flavor all the more. Instead of turning to my usual fresh lemon standby, I used a sweet apple and apple cider vinegar dressing. This is one of those great dishes that looks and tastes like you spent ages on it, but is actually really simple!

SERVES 4

1½ lbs (680 g) fresh asparagus

2 tbsp (30 ml) coconut or avocado oil

2 shallots, peeled and thinly sliced

½ tsp salt

¾ cup (180 ml) Double Apple Dressing (page 198)

ROAST: Preheat the oven to 400°F (205°C). Break off the woody ends of the asparagus with your hands. The stalks will naturally snap at the point where they are soft and edible—discard the thicker woody stems. Toss the asparagus with the oil, shallots and salt on a rimmed baking sheet lined with parchment paper. Spread the asparagus out on the baking sheet and roast until the asparagus is tender with a touch of color and the shallots are crispy, about 10-12 minutes.

DRIZZLE: Divide the roasted asparagus between plates or pile on a serving platter. Drizzle generously with the Double Apple Dressing and enjoy!

PLANTAIN CROQUETTES
WITH PANCETTA & RED ONION

Did you know that you can make the perfect croquette dough with just one ingredient and a little water? It's true! This recipe makes a simple dough from mashed plantains. Instead of the traditional ham filling, here I've used salty pancetta and sweet red onion to contrast the soft fluffy dough with crispy edges. This flavor combination is seriously good, but you could swap out the filling for so many other options—try using the Cuban Style Picadillo recipe (page 53).

MAKES 8

12 oz (340 g) plantains (about 2)
¼ cup (60 ml) water
4 oz (110 g) pancetta
½ cup (70 g) diced red onion
¼ tsp dried rosemary leaves

Coconut or avocado oil for frying

MIX: Bring a pan of salted water to a boil. Cut each plantain in half, then use a knife to cut a slit lengthways along the ridges of the plantain skin. Peel off the skin and discard it, using a knife to remove any stubborn pieces, if needed. Cut each plantain in half again and carefully drop the plantain pieces into the boiling water. Cover the pan with a lid and cook until the plantains are tender, about 35 minutes. Drain the cooked plantains and let them cool until they're no longer releasing steam before adding them to the bowl of a food processor. Pulse until the plantains are roughly mashed, then add the water. Process until a ball of dough is formed. Pinch some of the dough together with your fingers: if it sticks together, it's ready to use. If it's a little dry, add a little extra water a teaspoon at a time and process again.

COOK: While the plantains are boiling, make the filling. In a small skillet over medium heat, cook the pancetta until the fat is rendered and it just begins to crisp at the edges. Remove the pancetta with a slotted spoon and reserve for later. Reduce the heat a little and add the diced red onion and rosemary to the skillet and cook in the rendered pancetta fat, until the onions are soft, about 10 minutes. Mix the softened onions with the pancetta and allow to cool slightly.

FRY: Divide the dough into 8 equally-sized portions—using a ¼ cup (60 ml) scoop helps with this! Squeeze each portion of dough into a ball, then place it in a cupped hand. Use your other hand to flatten the ball into a round shape. Spoon a little of the pancetta filling into the middle of the flattened dough. Curl your hand around to start forming a ball, then pinch the edges of the dough together around the filling. Gently squeeze and press the filled dough into a round patty shape that is about 2½-inches (6-cm) wide. Repeat for the remaining dough and filling until you have 8 finished croquettes. Fill a skillet with enough oil to come halfway up the height of the croquettes. Heat the oil to 350°F (175°C) and carefully fry the croquettes in batches, flipping once, until each side is crispy and golden-brown, about 3–4 minutes per side. Transfer the cooked croquettes to a paper towel–lined plate to soak up any excess oil, then eat immediately!

WATERMELON GAZPACHO
WITH BASIL

Who says you need tomatoes to make gazpacho? Not me! Although I've used fresh watermelon as the base of this recipe, it's not sweet like you might expect. Instead, this gazpacho is decidedly savory, thanks to the red onion and fragrant fresh basil, with a little gentle heat from the radishes.

SERVES 4

3 cups (450 g) chopped seedless watermelon, in chunks

1 cup (140 g) red onion, chopped

3 tbsp (45 ml) lime juice

6 radishes, chopped in half

¼ cup (10 g) fresh basil leaves

Pinch of salt, to taste

BLEND: Add all ingredients to a blender and blend until smooth. Check the seasoning and add a little extra salt if you prefer.

CHILL: Refrigerate and chill the soup for at least 4 hours, or overnight. If I know I won't need my blender again, I'll pop the whole pitcher into the refrigerator so that the soup is easy to pour whenever I want it.

SPINACH-BLACKBERRY SALAD
WITH WARM BACON SAGE DRESSING

This is one of the classic salads I make often—there's something so satisfying about the combination of sweet tart blackberries and bacon. And for those who don't like to eat their greens—what's not to love about vitamins and minerals that just happen to be covered in warm bacon sage dressing?

SERVES 4

6 slices bacon

3 tbsp (45 ml) bacon fat (from cooking the bacon)

2 tbsp (30 ml) red wine vinegar

1 tbsp (15 ml) maple syrup

8 leaves fresh sage

8 cups (240 g) spinach leaves

6 oz (160 g) blackberries

¼ cup (40 g) finely sliced red onion

CRISP: In a large skillet, fry the bacon until crisp. Set the bacon aside to cool and remove the pan from the stovetop.

EMULSIFY: In a mini food processor, add 3 tablespoons (15 ml) of the rendered bacon fat from the skillet. Add the red wine vinegar, maple syrup and fresh sage—process until the dressing is combined and the sage is chopped finely.

ASSEMBLE: Divide the spinach between 4 plates and top each with the blackberries and red onion. Chop the cooked crisped bacon into bite-size pieces. Drizzle the plates with warm dressing and top with the bacon pieces. Serve immediately, while the bacon dressing is still warm.

ROASTED OKRA
WITH HOT & SOUR DIPPING SAUCE

Long ago, the only way I would eat okra was breaded and deep-fried. Preferably dunked in some dairy-laden dip. Yuck. The only other way I'd ever come across okra was in gumbo—where I found it disgustingly goopy. I'd put money on the fact that if you asked someone about why they don't like okra, their response would probably include the words "gross" and "slimy." But even resolute okra haters love okra when it's roasted! Why? The soluble fiber that makes okra not so pleasant when it's cut up and cooked normally doesn't come into contact with any water this way—which means you get deliciously browned crunchy okra, sans "slime." Be warned, though: Dipping the roasted okra in this hot & sour sauce actually makes okra addictive!

SERVES 4

FOR THE OKRA

1 lb (454 g) fresh okra

1 tbsp (15 ml) coconut or avocado oil

¼ tsp garlic powder

¼ tsp salt

FOR THE DIPPING SAUCE

¼ cup (60 ml) coconut cream

¼ cup (10 g) fresh cilantro leaves, finely chopped

2 tsp (10 ml) tamarind paste

2 tsp (4 g) ground ginger

2 tsp (10 ml) coconut aminos

¼ tsp garlic powder

ROAST: Preheat the oven to 450°F (230°C). Put the okra into a large bowl and toss together with the oil, garlic powder and salt. Line a baking sheet with parchment paper and spread the okra out in a single layer. Roast for 15–20 minutes, shaking the pan after the first 10 minutes, until the okra has lovely browned patches and is just tender with a little crunch. While the okra is roasting, make the dipping sauce.

MIX: In a bowl, whisk together all the ingredients for the dipping sauce. When the okra is roasted, serve it hot from the oven with the dipping sauce on the side.

NOTE: Tamarind paste is super sour! Add ½ teaspoon at a time if you've never used it before or don't want a really sour dipping sauce. You could also try substituting fresh lime juice, although that will need more juice and will result in a thinner sauce. If you don't want an especially hot dipping sauce, start off with 1 teaspoon of the ground ginger.

NOT CRAZY ABOUT COCONUT? Replace the coconut cream with 2 tablespoons (30 ml) of Eggless "Mayo" (page 196) and omit the coconut aminos. Add 1 teaspoon (5 ml) gluten-free fish sauce.

BALSAMIC-GLAZED MUSHROOMS
WITH KABOCHA SQUASH PUREE

This dish is a perfect pairing! Savory sautéed mushrooms glazed with balsamic vinegar, on top of a sweet but light kabocha squash puree. It's a little bit creamy and a little bit tangy! Eating a variety of mushrooms is a great way to boost your intake of minerals like selenium and potassium, too.

SERVES 4

1 medium kabocha squash, about 3½ lbs (1.6 kg)

3 tbsp (45 ml) duck fat, divided

1 cup (140 g) diced onion

2 cloves garlic, chopped

6 fresh sage leaves

¾ tsp salt, divided

1 lb (454 g) white or cremini mushrooms, sliced

2 tbsp (30 ml) balsamic vinegar

ROAST: Preheat the oven to 400°F (205°C). Carefully cut the kabocha squash in half and scrape out the seeds. Line a baking tray with parchment paper or foil and place the squash cut-side down onto the tray. Roast until the squash is tender when you pierce it with a fork, about 45–60 minutes. Set aside to cool slightly.

GLAZE: Add 2 tablespoons (30 ml) of the duck fat to a skillet over medium heat. Add the diced onion to the skillet and cook until softened, about 5 minutes, then add the garlic and sage leaves to the pan and cook for another minute or so. Transfer the onion, garlic and sage to a blender or food processor. Add the remaining duck fat to the pan, along with ¼ teaspoon of the salt and the sliced mushrooms. Cook for about 10 minutes, stirring occasionally, until the mushrooms are just tender. Pour in the balsamic vinegar and cook until the mushrooms are glazed, about 2–3 minutes. Remove the skillet from the heat and keep warm.

PUREE: Scoop out the roasted squash and add it to the blender or food processor along with the rest of the salt. Puree together until smooth. To serve, spread the kabocha squash puree on the bottom of a serving dish and pile the glazed mushrooms on top.

GERMAN POTATO SALAD
WITH BACON AND HERBS

You don't need mayo or goopy dressings to make a perfect potato salad. This version is deliciously tangy, yet fresh at the same time because it's full of herbs, too. White sweet potato works best here as it's nowhere near as sweet as the orange varieties. And what's not to love about adding bacon?

SERVES 8

2 lbs (900 g) white sweet potatoes

2 tsp (10 g) salt

¼ cup (60 ml) white wine vinegar

4 strips bacon

2 tbsp (30 ml) bacon fat

2 tbsp (30 ml) olive oil

2 tbsp (30 ml) apple cider vinegar

½ cup (70 g) diced red onion

¼ cup (30 g) finely chopped celery

2 tbsp (8 g) chopped chives

2 tbsp (10 g) minced flat-leaf parsley

2 tbsp (4 g) minced dill leaves

BOIL: Peel the sweet potatoes and chop them into bite-size pieces, about ½-inch (13-mm) each. Add the sweet potato chunks and salt to a saucepan and cover with water. Bring to a boil, then reduce the heat to an even simmer and cook until the potatoes are just tender, about 8 minutes. Drain the sweet potato and let it sit in the colander for a few minutes to let off steam.

MARINATE: Toss the hot sweet potato pieces in a bowl with the white wine vinegar. Let the potatoes marinate in and absorb the vinegar while they cool. While the potatoes are cooling, heat a skillet and fry the bacon until crispy. Transfer the bacon to a plate to cool and reserve 2 tablespoons (30 ml) of the bacon fat for later.

DRESS: Add the bacon fat, olive oil and apple cider vinegar to the bowl and toss the sweet potato to coat. Add the red onion, celery, chives, parsley and dill leaves and toss again to combine. Chop the bacon finely and sprinkle over the top of the salad before serving.

TIP: The salad will keep for several days in the fridge, but will need to be redressed with a little more olive oil as the potatoes will absorb the dressing over time.

SUMMER SQUASH SOUP
WITH LEMON

This soup is one of those sneaky recipes where the finished recipe turns out so much better than you would expect from the simple ingredients list. I based this recipe on the traditional Greek soup avgolemono—the name itself means "egg–lemon" because it is a broth-based lemon-flavored soup that is thickened by eggs. Instead of using gut-irritating whole eggs as thickener, I simmered some summer squash in the broth and blended that into the soup at the end. Extra veggies and an egg-free soup that's ready in under 30 minutes make this recipe a winner in my book.

MAKES 6 CUPS (1.4 L)

1 tbsp (15 ml) coconut or avocado oil

1 cup (140 g) diced onion

4 cups (450 g) summer squash, chopped into bite sized pieces (about 3 large)

2 cloves garlic, peeled and minced

½ tsp salt

4 cups (960 ml) Chicken Broth (page 225)

¼ cup + 2 tbsp (90 ml) lemon juice

1 tbsp (5 g) lemon zest

½ tsp ground turmeric

2 tbsp (30 ml) extra virgin olive oil

SOFTEN: Heat the coconut or avocado oil in a large saucepan and add the diced onion. Cook until softened, about 5 minutes. Add the summer squash, garlic and salt, stirring through the pan and cooking until the garlic is fragrant, about 1–2 minutes.

SIMMER: Add the chicken broth and increase the heat to bring the pan to a gentle simmer. Cook until the summer squash is tender, about 15 minutes. Add the lemon juice, lemon zest and turmeric. Remove the pan from the heat.

BLEND: Use an immersion blender to carefully blend the soup until smooth. Drizzle each bowl with a little extra virgin olive oil just before serving. This soup can be served hot or chilled.

APPLE & CUCUMBER SALAD
WITH SMOKED SALMON

Smoked salmon and cucumber is a classic pairing, often smothered in a creamy dressing. I've skipped that extra-heavy treatment here, livening things up with some tart apple and a lightly dressed salad with fresh herbs and salted capers for a little kick that cuts the richness of the salmon.

SERVES 4

2 cups (240 g) apple, peeled, cored and diced

2 tbsp (30 ml) lemon juice

4 cups (500 g) peeled, deseeded cucumber, chopped

¼ cup (60 ml) olive oil

1 shallot, minced finely

2 tbsp (4 g) chopped fresh chives

2 tsp (8 g) salted capers

Salt, to taste

8 oz (225 g) smoked salmon, sliced

TOSS: Add the diced apple and lemon juice to a bowl and toss to coat. Add the cucumber, olive oil, shallot, chives and capers, then stir to combine. Add salt, to taste. Divide the chopped salad between 4 plates and lay the smoked salmon on the side before serving.

INDIAN SPICED "RICE"
WITH LEMON AND RAISINS

Cauliflower can stand in admirably when it comes to recreating your favorite rice dish and is pretty tasty when it's seasoned well. Here I've made it the perfect curry accompaniment, spicing cauliflower, "rice", with plenty of ginger and cinnamon. Cauliflower "rice" makes a great substitute for inflammation-inducing grains, while still allowing you to enjoy the flavors you love. The vitamin K in cauliflower helps to regulate inflammatory responses, which means you're getting a nutritional kick *and* a tasty side dish, to boot!

SERVES 4

1½ lbs (680 g) cauliflower, cut into florets

3 tbsp (45 ml) coconut or avocado oil, divided

1 tsp (5 g) salt

1 cup (140 g) onion, diced

2 tsp (4 g) ground ginger

1 tsp (1 g) ground cinnamon

3 cloves garlic, minced

2 bay leaves

¼ cup (60 ml) lemon juice

¼ cup (60 ml) Chicken Broth (page 225)

1 tbsp (5 g) lemon zest

⅓ cup (65 g) dried raisins

¼ cup (10 g) fresh cilantro, minced

BAKE: Preheat the oven to 425°F (220°C). Working in batches, add the cauliflower florets to the bowl of a food processor and pulse until rice-size. Repeat until all cauliflower has been riced. Toss the riced cauliflower with 2 tablespoons (30 ml) of the oil and salt. Spread the riced cauliflower out on a lined baking tray and cook until tender, about 15-20 minutes.

SEASON: In a large skillet, add the remaining 1 tablespoon (15 ml) of oil. Soften the onion over low-medium heat until translucent, about 5 minutes. Add the ginger, cinnamon and garlic and cook for another 30 seconds, until fragrant. Remove the riced cauliflower from the oven and add to the skillet. Add the bay leaves and stir through the lemon juice, chicken broth, lemon zest, raisins and cilantro, then cook until the liquid has been absorbed and the rice is tender, about 5 minutes. Remove the bay leaves before serving.

SPRING SOUP
WITH CRISPY PROSCIUTTO

The gorgeous color of this soup is a little clue to just how healthy it is! It's packed with leafy greens and asparagus and keeps its vibrant hue because the vegetables are very lightly cooked before blending. You can switch this soup up with whatever spring greens you get from your CSA—this recipe is as forgiving as it is tasty! We love the slight bitterness the watercress adds to this recipe, but if you're not a fan, feel free to swap it for other milder greens.

SERVES 4

1 tbsp (15 ml) coconut or avocado oil

1 cup (140 g) diced onion

1 shallot, sliced finely

2 cloves garlic, chopped

1 lb (454 g) asparagus

1 packed cup (30 g) baby chard leaves

1 packed cup (30 g) baby spinach leaves

1 packed cup (30 g) watercress

3 cups (720 ml) Chicken Broth (page 225)

½ cup (120 g) mashed avocado

1 tbsp (15 ml) lemon juice

½ tsp salt

2–3 slices prosciutto

Chives, chopped for garnish

SOFTEN: Heat the oil over low-medium heat and add the diced onion, shallot and garlic. Cook until they begin to soften, but not brown, about 5 minutes. Snap any tough ends from the asparagus spears and cut them into 1-inch (2.5-cm) pieces. Add the asparagus pieces, baby chard, baby spinach and watercress to the pan and cook 5-10 minutes, until the spears are just starting to become tender and are bright green in color.

BLEND: Transfer the vegetables to a blender. Pour the chicken broth over and add the avocado, lemon juice and salt. Blend until completely smooth.

GARNISH: Preheat the broiler and grab a baking tray. Pour the blended soup back into the pan and cook until hot enough to serve. While the soup is warming, lay the prosciutto slices flat on the baking tray. Broil until they are darker in color and just crisp to the touch, 3–4 minutes. Chop the prosciutto slices into small pieces, like bacon bits—they will crisp up further as they cool. Divide the hot soup between bowls and garnish each with chopped chives and crispy prosciutto to serve.

CHILLED HONEYDEW SOUP
WITH CUCUMBER AND AVOCADO

This chilled soup is summer in a bowl! It's not only cool and refreshing from the combination of melon, cucumber and mint, but it's also got the good fats from the avocado that lend it a creamy consistency.

SERVES 4

---

3 cups (480 g) honeydew melon, cut into chunks

2 cups (270 g) peeled and chopped cucumber

⅔ cup (160 g) avocado

¼ cup (60 ml) lemon juice

¾ oz (20 g) fresh mint leaves

2 cloves garlic, peeled

Pinch of salt, to taste

BLEND: Add all ingredients to a blender and blend until smooth. Check seasoning and add a little extra salt if you prefer. If you would like to thin the soup a little, add a little water and reblend.

CHILL: Refrigerate and chill the soup for at least 4 hours, or overnight. If I know I won't need my blender again, I'll pop the whole pitcher into the refrigerator so that the soup is easy to pour whenever I want it.

CARROT & PARSNIP SALAD
WITH POMEGRANATE & MINT

Parsnips tend to be relegated to the standard winter preparations of roasting, baking and boiling. But these root vegetables are surprisingly tasty raw and are a good source of folate, which is needed for cell repair and growth. This salad pairs parsnips with carrots for a colorful variation on traditional carrot salads. The natural sweetness of the root vegetables pairs nicely with the zingy dressing, pomegranate and mint.

SERVES 4

½ lb (225 g) carrots, peeled
½ lb (225 g) parsnips, peeled
3 tbsp (45 ml) olive oil
1 tbsp (15 ml) white wine vinegar
1 tbsp (15 ml) lemon juice
1 tbsp (10 g) minced shallot
1 tsp honey
¼ cup (35 g) pomegranate arils
2 tbsp (6 g) chopped fresh mint leaves

PREP: Use a vegetable peeler to make flat "noodles" out of the carrots and parsnips, shaving thin strands off the vegetables lengthwise. Rotate the carrots and parsnips as you "peel" the vegetable ribbons to get the most from them. I don't like to peel into the tougher core, so I save those to drop into soups or to make broth. You could also coarsely grate the vegetables, if you prefer.

WHISK: In a small bowl or jug, whisk together the olive oil, white wine vinegar, lemon juice, shallot and honey. Toss the carrots and parsnips with the dressing in a large bowl.

TOP: Sprinkle the pomegranate arils and chopped fresh mint over the salad just before serving.

CIDER-BRAISED GREENS
WITH CRISPY BACON

Greens can often sound boring—I like to liven them up with some slightly unexpected flavors, like the gentle sweetness of apple cider and fragrant rosemary. I like to use a mix of hardier greens like kale along with more tender young leaves like baby Swiss chard and spinach—this gives a great contrast of texture that helps to liven up this nutritious side dish. Because calcium and vitamin C are pretty awesome, and eating a variety of greens is a great way to get more vitamins and minerals into your diet on a daily basis.

SERVES 6

3 slices bacon
1 cup (140 g) diced onion
1 lb (454 g) kale
2 small cloves garlic, minced
1 cup (240 ml) unsweetened apple cider
1 tbsp (15 ml) apple cider vinegar
½ lb (225 g) baby Swiss chard leaves
½ lb (225 g) fresh spinach
Salt, to taste

CRISP: Fry the bacon slices until crisp and set aside to cool. Keep 2 teaspoons (10 ml) of the rendered bacon fat and save the rest for future use.

SOFTEN: Add the diced onion to the pan with the bacon fat and cook until it is softened. While the onion is cooking, cut the kale leaves from the stems and slice finely. Chop the thick kale stems finely, so that the pieces are about the same size as the diced onion. Add the minced garlic to the pan and cook for another minute, until fragrant. Toss in the sliced kale leaves and stems and cook for about 5 minutes, until the kale starts to soften.

BRAISE: Add the apple cider vinegar, then cook until the kale is almost tender. Add the Swiss chard and spinach and salt, to taste. Cook until the lighter greens are just wilted and remove from the heat. Chop the cooled bacon into pieces and serve the greens with the bacon bits scattered over the top.

ROASTED SUNCHOKES
WITH APPLES & ONIONS

Sunchokes, or Jerusalem artichokes, make a great potato alternative and they're delicious roasted. Tossing them together with apples and onions adds a touch of natural sweetness and caramelization that is the perfect easy companion to almost any roast chicken or pork dish.

SERVES 4

1 lb (454 g) sunchokes

2 apples, peeled and cored

1 red onion

3 tbsp (45 ml) coconut or avocado oil

2 tsp (3 g) fresh rosemary, chopped

1 tsp salt

TOSS: Preheat the oven to 400°F (205°C). Scrub the sunchokes clean, leaving the skin on, and pat them dry. Cut into ¼-inch (6-mm) slices and add to a mixing bowl. Slice the apples into quarters and then into ¼-inch (6-mm) slices and add to the bowl. Remove the skin from the onion, then cut in half, and slice into ¼-inch (6-mm) thick half moons. Add them to the bowl along with the oil and toss to coat. Spread the oil-coated vegetables and fruit out in a single layer on a baking tray. Sprinkle with the rosemary and salt.

ROAST: Slide the baking tray into the oven and roast for 20 minutes. Turn the vegetables over and rearrange them in a single layer on the tray again. Return the tray to the oven and roast for another 10–15 minutes, until the sunchokes are tender and the onions are beginning to caramelize.

RADISH SALAD
WITH RADISH GREENS PESTO

Most people buying bunches of fresh radishes will discard the leaves without really thinking about it. I did that for years because I never even considered the possibility of eating them. It turns out that the radish leaves, like so many other leafy greens, are full of vitamin C, more so than the radishes themselves! They taste similar to arugula and make a fantastic pesto. Make sure to pick the radish bunches with the freshest, greenest-looking leaves: The thicker, tougher, darker-colored greens tend to be more bitter.

SERVES 4

2 large bunches radishes, with greens attached

¼ cup (20 g) unsweetened coconut flakes

¼ cup (10 g) fresh basil leaves

2 cloves garlic, peeled

¼ cup (60 ml) olive oil

¼ cup (60 ml) lemon juice

Pinch of fine sea salt

SLICE: Trim the radishes and remove the leaves from the stems. Keep the radishes and greens, discarding the stems. Wash well in a colander to remove any dirt and grit, then drain. Pat them dry. Use a mandoline to slice radishes thinly, about ⅛-inch (3-mm) thick. Lay overlapping slices on a serving plate and set aside.

BLEND: In a food processor, add the radish greens, coconut flakes, basil and garlic. Process until the radish greens are roughly chopped and the garlic minced. Add the olive oil, lemon juice and salt. Process until you have a smooth pesto. Serve drizzled over the sliced radishes, with an extra drizzle of extra-virgin olive oil to finish, if you like.

NOT CRAZY ABOUT COCONUT? You can omit the coconut flakes, which will give you a slightly thinner pesto.

GREEK "COUSCOUS" SALAD
WITH OREGANO DRESSING

This grainless version of a couscous salad is packed with classic Greek flavors—a double whammy of fragrant oregano, some zing from the lemon and plenty of olives to go around. Its lightness makes it the perfect companion to plenty of dishes, especially grilled meats. Take a batch to your next potluck BBQ and no one will mind about the missing grains.

SERVES 6

FOR THE DRESSING

½ cup + 2 tbsp (150 ml) olive oil

¼ cup (60 ml) red wine vinegar

2 tbsp (30 ml) lemon juice

2 tbsp (6 g) fresh oregano leaves

2 tsp (2 g) dried oregano leaves

2 cloves garlic

2 anchovy fillets

FOR THE SALAD

1 lb (454 g) cauliflower florets

2 cups (250 g) English cucumber

½ cup (80 g) kalamata olives

2 cups (280 g) diced red onion

2 tbsp (5 g) flat-leaf parsley, chopped

BLEND: Add all the dressing ingredients to a blender and combine. Reserve for later.

TOSS: Cut the cauliflower into florets and, working in batches, add them to the bowl of a food processor. Pulse the cauliflower until it is broken down into "couscous" sized pieces. Add the cauliflower "couscous" to a large bowl. Chop the cucumber into bite-size pieces and roughly chop the olives. Add all the ingredients to the bowl, along with the dressing, then toss to combine. Add salt, to taste, if needed. This salad can be eaten straightaway, but is even better when left to marinate for a few hours.

GARLIC-LOVERS ROASTED BEETS
WITH LEMON ZEST AND THYME

Beets. For some reason, they remind me of school lunches, where the salad bar was laden with untouched bowls of purple cubes. For years I couldn't bear to try a dish with beets in it. Which is a shame, since not only are they beautifully colorful, they're full of good things: vitamin C, calcium, manganese and iron, to name a few! This oven-roasting method means the beets are perfectly tender, with a hint of lemon and herbs. The real showstopper, though, is the garlic: it caramelizes and crisps on top to make crunchy nuggets of garlicky goodness.

SERVES 6

1½ lbs (675 g) beets

3 tbsp (45 ml) coconut or avocado oil

4 cloves garlic, roughly chopped

1 tsp (2 g) lemon zest

1 tsp (1 g) fresh thyme leaves

½ tsp salt

¼ cup (60 ml) Chicken Broth (page 225)

SLICE: Preheat the oven to 400°F (205°C). Peel the beets and cut off the tops. Use a mandoline to carefully slice the beets into ⅛-inch (3-mm) rounds.

LAYER: Grease a 10-inch (25-cm) cast-iron skillet with a little of the oil. Layer the beet slices in the skillet so that they overlap each other, in concentric circles. There will be 2–3 layers, depending upon the size of your beets. In another small pan, melt the rest of the rest of the oil over low heat. Add the garlic, lemon zest, thyme and salt, and cook until the garlic is fragrant and beginning to soften, but not brown. Carefully pour the seasoned oil over the top of the layered beets. Pour the chicken broth over and cover the skillet with a layer of foil, making a hole in the top for steam to escape.

ROAST: Cook the beets for 40 minutes. Remove and discard the foil, then return the beets to the oven and roast for 10-15 minutes, until the beets are just tender and the garlic has crisped.

WATERCRESS SALAD
WITH AVOCADO AND BASIL

This is my absolute favorite green salad: watercress and creamy avocado, lightly dressed and topped off with crispy-crunchy garlic crouton-a-likes! The combination of greens and good healthy fats is a winner.

SERVES 4

4 cups (120g) watercress

1 avocado, pit removed and thinly sliced

4 green onions

¼ cup (10 g) fresh basil leaves

Extra-virgin olive oil and fresh lemon juice, to taste

⅓ cup (15 g) Crunchy Salad Topper (page 223)

ASSEMBLE: Divide the watercress evenly between plates and top with the sliced avocado. Slice up the green onions and basil and scatter those over the plates. Drizzle with extra-virgin olive oil and lemon juice, to taste. Sprinkle each plate with the crunchy salad topper and serve straightaway—could salad get any easier?!

SAUTÉED RAPINI
WITH GARLIC AND SAUSAGE

This is a great side dish that comes together quickly. Rapini, or broccoli rabe, is a bitter green similar to mustard or turnip greens and is a great source of calcium and vitamin C. This recipe adds lots of flavor by sautéing the rapini with garlic and the rendered fat from sausage crumbles. The sweetness of the garlic and the richness of the browned sausage balance the robust flavor of the rapini perfectly.

SERVES 4

1¼ lb (565 g) bunch of rapini
4 oz (110 g) pork sausage (see note)
2 tbsp (30 ml) coconut or avocado oil
8 cloves of garlic, minced

COOK: Trim the rapini, removing and discarding the thick lower stems. Slice the rapini into 1-inch (2.5-cm) thick ribbons. Rinse the rapini and drain in a colander, setting it aside for now. In a large skillet over medium heat, crumble the pork sausage into the pan and cook for 5 minutes. Use a spatula to break the sausage up into smaller crumbles and toss the crumbles so that they brown evenly. Continue to cook until the sausage crumbles are golden-brown and cooked through, another 3–5 minutes. Remove the sausage crumbles from the pan with a slotted spoon and reserve them for later.

SAUTE: Add the oil to the skillet you cooked the sausage in and reduce the heat to low. Add the minced garlic to the pan and cook until the garlic is fragrant and just beginning to take on color, about 1 minute, stirring a few times to prevent burning. Add the rapini to the pan and toss in the garlic-scented oil. Sauté until the rapini is wilted but not overcooked, about 3–4 minutes. Add the sausage back to the pan and stir it through the rapini. Cook for another minute or so, until the sausage is warmed, then serve immediately.

NOTE: If you cannot find AIP-friendly sausage, use the seasoning blend in the Slow Cooker Breakfast Meatloaf (page 23) and add it to ground pork to make your own.

PURPLE SLAW
WITH FENNEL AND DILL

Unlike typical mayo-heavy coleslaw recipes, there's no soggy cabbage here! This slaw is light, zippy and super crunchy from first to last bite.

SERVES 4

½ lb (225 g) red cabbage

1 cup (85 g) thinly sliced fennel bulb

1 cup (85 g) thinly sliced red onion

2 tbsp (30 ml) olive oil

2 tbsp (30 ml) lemon juice

1 tbsp (15 ml) apple cider vinegar

1 tbsp (4 g) minced fennel leaves

1 tbsp (6 g) minced fresh dill

½ tsp salt

2 tbsp (2 g) chopped fennel fronds

2 tsp (2 g) dried dill

MARINATE: Use a mandoline to slice the cabbage thinly. Cut the fennel root in half and slice thinly with the mandolin, then do the same with the red onion. Toss the cabbage, fennel and red onion in a bowl with the remaining ingredients. You can serve the slaw immediately or refrigerate it, covered, overnight for the flavors to all meld together.

WHIPPED SWEET POTATOES
WITH PARSNIPS AND ROSEMARY

Sweet potatoes get all the Paleo-friendly carb glory and they make fantastically fluffy mash. But since they are naturally so sweet, I like to mix 'em up a bit and throw them together with some parsnips to make the perfect goes-with-everything mash. Parsnips are just the thing to mellow out the sweetness of the sweet potatoes and they make a super-creamy mash. I like to add a little bacon or duck fat for a subtle smoky flavor and a hint of rosemary for a perfect root vegetable side dish.

SERVES 4

1½ lbs (680 g) sweet potatoes

1 lb (454 g) parsnips

2 tbsp (30 ml) bacon or duck fat

¼ cup (60 ml) coconut milk

1 tsp (5 g) salt

1 tsp (1 g) dried rosemary

SIMMER: Peel the sweet potatoes and parsnips. Chop the sweet potatoes into 1-inch (2.5-cm) chunks and slice the parsnips into ½-inch (12-mm) rounds. Put the vegetables in a saucepan and add enough water to just cover them. Bring the pan to the boil and then reduce the heat to a simmer, cooking the vegetables until tender, about 15 minutes.

WHIP: When the sweet potatoes and parsnips are fork tender, remove the saucepan from the heat and drain them in a colander. Let them sit in the colander for a few minutes, allowing the steam to dissipate—this helps get rid of any extra moisture that will make your mash gummy. When the sweet potatoes and parsnips have cooled slightly and the steam has dissipated, add about half of them to the bowl of a food processor. Add the fat and process until a rough mash is formed. Add the rest of the sweet potatoes and parsnips, along with the coconut milk, salt and crushed rosemary. Process, scraping down the sides of the bowl a few times as necessary, until you have a smooth and creamy whipped mash. Pair this mash with any of your favorite comfort food dishes!

NOT CRAZY ABOUT COCONUT? Omit the coconut milk and add 2 tablespoons (30 ml) of Chicken Broth (page 225).

HOW TO DO DESSERT

When it comes to sweet treats, I like to keep things simple. These days, my idea of a dessert is usually fresh berries with a little coconut milk or whipped coconut cream. That's why this chapter is a small collection of healthy (and mostly no-cook) desserts that don't take much time or energy to whip up. They won't cost you a small fortune in strange ingredients, either! Instead, these desserts are fruit based, minimally sweetened and often paired with healthy fats like avocado and coconut to make them satisfying enough that a small serving is just enough to hit the spot.

BALSAMIC ROASTED STRAWBERRY POPSICLES
WITH COCONUT MILK

Roasting fruit is always a great idea because it gives such a delicious concentrated and rich fruit flavor to a dish. Here I've gone one step further by adding balsamic vinegar to the mix, which brings out the natural sweetness of the strawberries even more! Swirling the strawberries with rich and creamy coconut milk makes the perfect popsicle that is a fun play on the classic pairing of strawberries and cream.

MAKES 8 POPSICLES

1 lb (454 g) strawberries
¼ cup (60 ml) balsamic vinegar
2 tbsp (30 ml) honey
2 tbsp (4 g) chopped basil
1½ cups (360 ml) coconut milk

ROAST: Preheat the oven to 400°F (205°C). Hull the strawberries and chop them roughly. Put them in a baking dish and toss them with the balsamic vinegar and honey. Roast for 30 minutes, until the juices released by the strawberries are bubbling and the fruit is soft.

BLEND: Transfer the roasted strawberries and all the pan juices to a blender. Add the basil and blend until smooth.

SWIRL: Spoon about 2 tablespoons (30 ml) of the roasted strawberry mixture into the bottom of each popsicle mold, then divide the coconut milk evenly between the molds. Top the popsicles with the remaining strawberry mixture. Freeze the popsicles for 30 minutes before sliding a popsicle stick into each mold. Return to the freezer and freeze until solid, at least 4 hours. Run the popsicle mold under a little warm water to release the popsicles when you're ready to eat them.

SPICED BANANA-CAROB PUDDING
WITH CRISPY BACON

If banana pudding and a Mexican hot chocolate made an AIP-friendly dessert love child, I'm pretty sure this is what would happen. This creamy pudding is full of good fats and doesn't rely on any kind of "milk" product because of the avocado and is naturally sweetened by banana, so no added sugars are needed. Just to go a little over the top, I've added cinnamon, a pinch of salt and bacon. Because, bacon.

SERVES 4

2 cups (480 g) mashed banana

¾ cup (160 g) mashed avocado

¼ cup (24 g) raw carob powder

2½ tsp (3 g) ground cinnamon

¾ tsp ground ginger

¼ tsp salt

1–2 slices bacon, cooked and cut into pieces

¼ cup (60 ml) coconut cream (optional, to serve)

PUREE: Add the banana, avocado, carob, cinnamon, ginger and salt to a blender or food processor. Puree until the mixture is smooth.

CHILL: Divide the pudding between 4 ramekins or glasses and smooth the tops with the back of a spoon. Chill for 1 hour. Top the puddings with a sprinkle of bacon pieces just before serving. If you like, you can also top the puddings with some chilled coconut cream for a little extra-decadent deliciousness!

"SOFT SERVE" SUNDAE
WITH SALTED CARAMELIZED PLANTAINS

This one ingredient banana "soft serve" is super easy and you don't need a fancy ice cream machine to make it! Here it's part of a fruit-based sundae that still tastes decadent because of the way it combines salty and sweet flavors. Cooking the plantains in bacon fat gives a nice smokiness and using ripe plantains means that you don't need to add any extra processed forms of sugar to make them caramelize beautifully.

SERVES 4

4 cups (500 g) frozen banana chunks or slices

2 ripe plantains, sliced into 4 lengthwise

2 tbsp (30 ml) bacon fat

Pinch of sea salt

¼ cup (30 g) Crunchy Sundae Topper (page 223)

1 tbsp (15 ml) raw honey (optional)

PROCESS: Add the frozen banana chunks to the bowl of a food processor. Process on low until the consistency is similar to soft-serve. Once the frozen bananas are smooth, don't overprocess or the "ice cream" will begin to melt. Transfer to a container and place in the freezer.

CARAMELIZE: Peel the plantains and slice them in half lengthwise. Place the pieces flat-side down on the cutting board and carefully slice each piece in half again lengthwise so that you have 8 long pieces of plantain in total. Heat a large skillet over medium heat with the bacon fat. Working in batches, lay the plantain slices in the pan and sprinkle with sea salt. Cook on each side until they begin to brown and caramelize, about 3–4 minutes per side. Remove the plantains from the pan and set them aside for now.

ASSEMBLE: Remove the banana "ice cream" from the freezer and use an ice cream scoop to divide it into 4 portions. Divide the caramelized plantains between serving dishes and top the sundae with the crushed crunchy sundae topper. If you like, drizzle each plate with a little raw honey before serving.

LAYERED COCONUT MOUSSE
WITH MANDARIN ORANGE

This mousse is deliciously rich and creamy because it uses a mixture of coconut cream and coconut milk to mimic the high fat content of traditional mousse, without needing to use eggs. Coconut cream is high in healthy saturated fat, which means that it helps you feel full and satisfied. The fresh mandarin juice provides vitamin C as well as a great tangy counterpart to the rich mousse. That makes these layered mousses decadent and nutritious!

SERVES 4

FOR THE BOTTOM LAYER
1 tsp (2 g) gelatin powder
2 tbsp (30 ml) water
½ cup (120 ml) mandarin juice
1 tbsp (15 ml) raw honey

FOR THE MOUSSE
2 tsp (5 g) gelatin powder
¼ cup (60 ml) water
1½ cups (360 ml) coconut cream
½ cup (120 ml) coconut milk
2 tbsp (30 ml) raw honey
1 tbsp (5 g) mandarin zest
½ tsp alcohol-free vanilla extract

TO MAKE THE BOTTOM LAYER

DISSOLVE: Sprinkle the gelatin powder over the water in a bowl. Set aside while the gelatin blooms. In a small saucepan over very low heat, gently warm the mandarin juice and honey. Add the bloomed gelatin and stir until the gelatin has combined and there are no lumps.

CHILL: Divide the liquid between 4 ramekins. Refrigerate the ramekins until the mixture has set, about 2 hours.

TO MAKE THE MOUSSE

DISSOLVE: Sprinkle the gelatin powder over the water in a bowl. Set aside while the gelatin blooms. In a small saucepan over very low heat, gently warm all the remaining ingredients. Add the bloomed gelatin and stir until the gelatin has combined and there are no lumps. Use a fine-mesh sieve to pour the mousse mixture into the jug of a blender and remove the mandarin zest. Discard the zest.

LAYER: Put the blender jug into the refrigerator and chill until cool to the touch, about 10 minutes. Remove the blender jug from the refrigerator and blend the mousse mixture on high for about 30 seconds to introduce air bubbles and make sure that the mixture is fully emulsified. Divide the mousse mixture evenly between the chilled ramekins and refrigerate until set, about 3 hours. Top each mousse with thin slices of mandarin orange just before serving.

PEACH GRANITA
WITH THYME AND GINGER

Every time I make granita, I think of the slushies I used to love as a kid! This version is definitely for grown-ups since it pairs the natural sweetness of peaches with a refreshingly clean hint of herbs!

SERVES 6

12 oz (340 g) peeled and pitted peaches

1½ cups (360 ml) water

2 tsp (10 ml) fresh lime juice

2 tsp (2 g) fresh thyme leaves

1 tsp (2 g) fresh minced ginger

Pinch salt

BLEND: Add all ingredients to a blender and puree until smooth.

FREEZE: Pour the granita into a freezer-safe dish. Freeze for 3 hours, scraping the mixture with a fork every hour to make fluffy, icy chunks. Spoon into glasses to serve.

MANGO SORBET
WITH MINT

The great thing about this dessert is that it comes together in about a minute and doesn't require an ice cream maker! Frozen mango creates a lovely creamy texture when it's blended, so there's no need for dairy products or even coconut milk to stand in for them. A tasty frozen treat without any waiting around—now that tastes like winning!

MAKES 8 SCOOPS

17.5 oz (500 g) frozen mango chunks

½ cup (120 ml) filtered water

¼ cup (60 ml) fresh lime juice (about 2 limes)

4 sprigs fresh mint, leaves only (about 25)

¼ cup (60 ml) raw honey (optional)

PULSE: Add all the ingredients to a powerful blender—it needs to be capable of crushing ice or the frozen mango chunks will not blend. Pulse until the mango chunks have been broken up and crushed.

BLEND: Scrape down the sides of the blender, then blend again until the sorbet is just combined. Don't run the blender any longer than you need to, or the blender will generate enough heat to melt the sorbet. Serve immediately, or, if you like a firmer texture, transfer the sorbet to a freezer-safe container and freeze for 30 minutes—1 hour before serving.

ADD A LITTLE EXTRA

Sometimes, food just needs a little extra...oomph. If you're crazy for condiments, you might find yourself fighting to add flavor when nightshades and seed spices are out. Buh-bye, ketchup and mustard! See you later, hot sauce! And as for BBQ sauce or salsa...forget about it! Right?

Well, I get to be the bearer of good news here. There are plenty of ways to bring back bold flavors without having to trigger an autoimmune flare by eating non-compliant dips, sauces or seasonings. This chapter is full of things that you can dip, dunk, spread, pour or slather on your meals, not to mention simple methods for making your own flavorful and nutritious Best Broths (page 224), or your own Flavored Finishing Salts (page 216). We're bringing even more flavor back with Taco Seasoning (page 219) and Thai "Curry" Paste (page 202). Yes, they're possible on the AIP! I've even got a kickass BBQ Sauce (page 201) for you that can be used exactly like traditional BBQ sauce recipes *and* a No-Nightshade Salsa (page 205). You're not going to want to miss out on all these little extras, and more!

EGGLESS "MAYO"

This a super-easy and versatile recipe that gives a whipped, creamy tasting "mayo" without any eggs...or weird egg replacers. You can use it as is, or flavor it with extra herbs as you wish and it makes an excellent base for dipping sauces, like the Garlic "Mayo" Dipping Sauce (page 136) or the Preserved Lemon & Chive "Mayo" (page 100). It will keep in the fridge for a week or so—just take it out a few minutes ahead of time and give it a good stir to ensure that it is spreadable.

MAKES 1 CUP (236 ML)

¾ cup (180 ml) sustainably sourced palm shortening

½ cup (120 ml) avocado oil

2 tbsp (30 ml) lemon juice

Pinch of salt

BLEND: You have to use an immersion blender for this recipe, as that is what gives the "mayo" its smooth whipped texture. Add all of the ingredients to a mason jar or the measuring and blending jar that came with your immersion blender. Blend everything together until smooth...and that's it! Chill the "mayo" for about an hour before using.

DOUBLE APPLE DRESSING
WITH LEMON AND SHALLOT

This dressing is made with a combination of both fresh apples and apple cider vinegar, making a refreshingly bright, sweet-tart dressing that doesn't need any added sweetener. Choose a raw, organic, unfiltered apple cider vinegar that comes with the "mother" to get the prebiotic benefits that help improve digestion.

MAKES 1½ CUPS (360 ML)

1½ cups (190 g) chopped, peeled and cored sweet apples
½ cup (120 ml) olive oil
3 tbsp (45 ml) apple cider vinegar
2 tbsp (30 ml) lemon juice
2 tbsp (20 g) shallot, minced
Pinch of salt

BLEND: Add all ingredients to a high-power blender and blend on high until smooth. Use the dressing on salads, as a vegetable dip or as a sauce for meat and vegetables. You can keep this in the fridge for several days.

SMOKY AVOCADO SPREAD
WITH BACON FAT

This is a great way to amp up flavor on a variety of dishes because it's packed with creaminess from the avocado and a lovely smoky flavor from the bacon fat. I like to use it as a burger topping, like on the Duck Fat Burgers (page 50), once it's chilled or as a dip for veggies if I'm too lazy to chill it!

MAKES ¼ CUP (180 ML)

½ cup (120 g) mashed avocado

¼ cup (60 ml) rendered, strained and cooled bacon fat

2 tbsp (30 ml) lemon juice

Pinch of salt, to taste

BLEND: Use an immersion blender to combine all ingredients except salt until smooth. Taste and season with extra salt as needed. Can be used straightaway but the texture will be closer to a sauce. If you refrigerate the spread for an hour or more, it will thicken up to more of a guacamole texture.

BBQ SAUCE
SWEET *AND* TANGY

When I first started following the AIP, I assumed that good BBQ was something I couldn't enjoy again for a long, long time. I tried making plenty of fruit-based recipes, but they never quite had the right flavors—and they didn't behave like "real" BBQ sauce. They didn't react well to high heat and, in fact, usually burned, which meant they could only be added to meals at the table and couldn't be cooked with. Well, this BBQ sauce is not only nightshade- and seed spice-free, but it looks like, tastes like and acts like BBQ Sauce. It really, really does.

MAKES 2 CUPS (480 ML)

1 cup (140 g) yellow onion

½ cup (120 ml) apple cider vinegar

4 oz (120 ml) unsweetened apple sauce

¼ cup + 2 tbsp (90 ml) coconut aminos

¼ cup + 2 tbsp (90 ml) honey

¼ cup (60 ml) balsamic vinegar

¼ cup (60 ml) pumpkin puree

2 tbsp (30 ml) molasses

2 cloves garlic

2 tbsp + 1 tsp (14 g) ground ginger

1 tbsp (15 g) mesquite smoked salt, or similar

1 tsp (5 ml) gluten-free fish sauce

¼ cup (60 ml) bacon fat

SIMMER: Add all ingredients except the bacon fat to a food processor or blender and puree until totally smooth, scraping down the sides a few times as needed. Pour the blended ingredients into a saucepan and heat gently until the BBQ sauce comes to a simmer. Add the bacon fat and stir to combine. Reduce the heat so the sauce continues to gently simmer for 10–15 minutes, stirring frequently, while the sauce reduces and thickens. Don't worry about the foam you will see on top of the sauce when you first begin to cook it: That will disappear as the sauce is cooked. The BBQ sauce will darken to a rich brown as it cooks. If you would like your BBQ sauce with a little extra tang, add extra apple cider vinegar, to taste, once the sauce has simmered and cook for a further 5 minutes. Use straightaway or pour the BBQ sauce carefully into jars to cool. It will keep in the fridge for at least a week.

NOT CRAZY ABOUT COCONUT? Omit the coconut aminos and add 2 tablespoons (30 ml) of fish sauce and an extra 1 tablespoon (15 ml) of balsamic vinegar.

THAI GREEN "CURRY" PASTE

Traditionally, Thai curry paste is made with a mortar and pestle, but this version cuts the hard work by using a food processor to whip up the paste. This green "curry" paste has no nightshades but is full of punchy flavors that are light and refreshing yet robust enough to stand up to the richness of coconut milk when used as a curry, soup or marinade base.

MAKES ABOUT 1 CUP (240 ML)

½ packed cup (20 g) Thai basil

⅓ packed cup (15 g) cilantro leaves and stems

1 oz (30 g) lemongrass, sliced finely

2 tbsp (30 ml) lime juice

2 cloves garlic

3 tbsp (15 g) grated ginger

2 tbsp (12 g) dried shrimp

2 tbsp (30 ml) water

2 tbsp (15 ml) honey

1 shallot, chopped

1 tsp (5 ml) gluten-free fish sauce

1 tsp (5 g) coarse sea salt

1 tsp (2 g) ground ginger

BLEND: Add all ingredients to a food processor or blender and process, scraping down the sides several times, until you have an almost completely smooth paste. The paste will be spreadable and easy to spoon, but not quite as smooth as commercially produced pastes. Use immediately or store in the fridge for up to a week. Can be stored in the freezer for 6 months.

USE: This as the base for marinades or curries. Add to stir-fries or rub on meats before grilling or roasting.

NO-NIGHTSHADE SALSA
WITH CUCUMBER, LIME & CILANTRO

Mr. Meatified didn't think I could pull this one off—I mean, what's salsa without tomatoes and jalapeños? Well, guess what? You don't need either of those ingredients to make a fantastic fresh salsa that's perfect for dipping and dunking. We like to make this vegetable-filled salsa a little chunky, which is why I pulse the onions and cucumber in at the very end—if you like your salsa smooth, just throw it all together at once.

MAKES 1 CUP (240 ML)

2 oz (55 g) canned beets, drained

2 tbsp (30 ml) pumpkin puree

2 tbsp (30 ml) water

1 tbsp (15 ml) lime juice

2 tsp (10 ml) olive oil

½ tsp Taco Seasoning (page 219)

½ cup (70 g) diced red onion

¾ cup (135 g) peeled and de-seeded cucumber, chopped

⅓ cup (14 g) fresh cilantro leaves

Salt, to taste

BLEND: Chop the beets into pieces and add them to the bowl of a mini food processor along with the pumpkin puree, water, lime juice, olive oil and Taco Seasoning. Pulse until the mixture is just combined, not completely smooth. Add the onion, cucumber and cilantro and pulse a few more times to make a chunky salsa. Add salt to taste. You can eat this straightaway, but the salsa is at its best when it has been chilled for a few hours and the flavors have had time to marry together.

CREAMY GREEN ONION DRESSING
WITH LEMON

Traditionally, "creamy" dressings are made with a variety of inflammatory dairy products. This recipe substitutes in coconut cream, which gives the same decadent texture because of its high fat content. Unlike the fat in dairy products, however, the type of fat found in coconut cream (medium-chain triglycerides) has been shown to actually reduce inflammation, making it a great choice for most people on the AIP.

MAKES ¾ CUP (180 ML)

⅔ cup (160 ml) coconut cream
⅔ cup (45 g) green onions, chopped
1 tbsp (15 ml) lemon juice
¼ tsp garlic powder
Pinch of salt

BLEND: In a food processor, pulse all the ingredients together until combined. Can be stored in the fridge for a few days, but any leftovers will solidify in the refrigerator, so blend the dressing again or take it out from the refrigerator 30 minutes before using and stir it through to make it pourable again.

CREAMY ARTICHOKE DIP
WITH SPINACH

This dip doesn't need dairy or coconut products to replicate the creaminess of this much-beloved appetizer. In fact, this recipe uses even more vegetables than normal to create the smooth, delicious, scoopable texture... which means we just won't tell any tiny humans just how good for them this recipe really is! This recipe is such a crowd-pleaser that I usually make it in a double batch, like I did here, so feel free to scale the recipe down to suit you, if needed.

MAKES 1¾ CUPS (420 G)

1 tbsp (15 ml) coconut or avocado oil

⅓ cup (45 g) diced onion

2 cloves garlic, minced

1 cup (120 g) peeled summer squash

¾ cup (180 ml) Chicken Broth (page 225)

6 oz (170 g) drained jarred artichoke hearts

2 tbsp (8 g) nutritional yeast

½ tsp ground mace

6 oz (170 g) package of frozen spinach, thawed

SOFTEN: Add the oil to a saucepan over medium heat. Add the diced onion and garlic to the pan while you peel and chop the summer squash. Cut the summer squash into pieces that are the same size as the diced onion, then add to the pan and stir to coat with the oil. Cook until the squash is tender, stirring occasionally so the squash doesn't brown, about 10 minutes.

BLEND: Transfer the softened vegetables to a blender and add the chicken broth. Gently squeeze the artichoke hearts to release any excess water before you weigh them out. Add the artichoke hearts, nutritional yeast and mace to the blender—process until you have a thick, smooth, "creamy" sauce.

SIMMER: Pour the sauce back into the saucepan and return to the stove top at a low heat. Drain the spinach and squeeze out any excess water, then chop finely. Stir the frozen spinach into the sauce and simmer until the dip is warmed through. The dip probably won't need any additional salt because of the artichoke hearts, but taste now and add any extra salt if you wish. Serve the dip warm and enjoy. Try pairing it with Pita Wedges (page 222).

SPEEDY CARAMELIZED ONIONS
WITH THYME

You don't need to spend hours over the stove to get rich, delicious caramelized onions—here's how I do it in about 30 minutes! Caramelized onions can add a sumptuous boost of flavor to so many things, like my Sweet Potato Gratin (page 143). Try adding them to beef or bison dishes, into dips or to simple vegetable sides.

MAKES ABOUT 1 CUP (240 G)

6 cups (600 g) onions

2 tbsp (30 ml) coconut or avocado oil

4–6 sprigs fresh thyme

1 tsp (5 g) salt

½ cup (120 ml) Beef Broth (page 224), divided

1 tbsp (15 ml) balsamic vinegar

COOK: Chop each onion in half through the root and remove the outside skin. Slice each half into thin crescents, about ⅛-inch (3-mm) thick. Heat a large skillet over medium-high heat and pour in the oil. Toss the sliced onions to coat in the oil, add the thyme sprigs and sprinkle with salt. Cook the onions for 15 minutes, stirring occasionally so that the onions begin to brown rather than burn. Pour in half of the beef broth and scrape up the fond from the bottom of the pan with a spatula. Cook for another 5 minutes, until all the broth is cooked off, then repeat with the remaining beef broth and cook for another 5 minutes. Drizzle the balsamic vinegar into the pan and cook for another 5 minutes, until the onions are sticky and caramelized. Remove the thyme sprigs before using in your recipes.

GRILLED PINEAPPLE GUACAMOLE
WITH RED ONION AND CILANTRO

Most guacamole recipes call for tomatoes or jalapeños, but this Grilled Pineapple Guacamole shows you how to make a flavorful avocado dip without those gut-irritating nightshades. This is a quick and easy accompaniment to lots of dishes, from seafood and chicken to pork but it pairs especially well with Pork Belly Carnitas (page 39).

SERVES 4

3.5 oz (100 g) fresh pineapple

1 tbsp (15 ml) coconut or avocado oil

2-3 avocados

¼ cup (35 g) diced red onion

¼ cup (10 g) fresh cilantro leaves, chopped

1 tbsp (15 ml) fresh lime juice (about ½ lime)

Pinch of Taco Seasoning (page 219)

Smoked salt, to taste

GRILL: Cut the ends from a fresh pineapple and discard them. Stand the pineapple up on a flat end and carefully slice away the skin, working your way around the pineapple until all the skin is removed. Cut two ½-inch (1.5-cm) rings from the pineapple and reserve the rest for another recipe. Preheat a cast-iron grill pan over high heat. Coat the grill pan with a little coconut or avocado oil to prevent sticking. Lay the pineapple on the hot grill pan and cook for about 15 minutes or so per side, rotating 45 degrees halfway through, until the pineapple has some nice charred grill marks. Set the pineapple slices aside to cool. Cut the avocados in half and discard the pits. Leave the skin intact and place the avocados, cut side down, on the grill pan. Cook, rotating once by 45 degrees to get extra grill marks, for about 5 minutes, until the avocados are lightly charred.

MIX: Dice the grilled pineapple, discarding the tough inner core, and set to one side. Carefully scoop the avocado into a bowl and mash with a fork, leaving some chunks of avocado for texture. Add the red onion, cilantro, lime juice and Taco Seasoning, stirring to just combine everything together. Fold in the grilled pineapple chunks gently so that they do not get mashed into the guacamole. Taste and add smoked salt, to taste. Best when eaten straightaway.

CHERRY SAUCE
WITH THYME

This quick and easy sauce goes fantastically with roasted meats and takes only a few minutes to whip up. The simple fruit base avoids unnecessary added sugars and the cherries give a great flavor without having to use inflammatory nightshades. This goes perfectly with all kinds of roasted meats and is great for livening up lunchtime cold cuts!

MAKES ABOUT 10 OZ (280 ML)

3 cups (400 g) pitted dark cherries

½ cup (120 ml) unsweetened apple sauce

1 tbsp (15 ml) coconut or avocado oil

2 tbsp (30 ml) balsamic vinegar

2 tsp (2 g) dried thyme leaves

¼ tsp salt

SIMMER: Add all ingredients to a saucepan and simmer over medium heat so that it bubbles continuously. Stir occasionally until thickened, about 10 minutes.

ZUCCHINI-LEEK SPREAD
WITH SHALLOTS AND LEMON

I love this stuff! This recipe is a great way to use up bountiful squash in the summer—and it can be used so many different ways. It's great as a topper for chicken or steak, can be pureed into a delicious dip and can even work as a stuffing, like in the recipe for Prosciutto-Wrapped Trout (page 216).

MAKES 2 CUPS (480 G)

2 lbs (900 g) zucchini

½ tsp salt

2 leeks

2 shallots

¼ cup (60 ml) coconut or avocado oil

Zest of 2 lemons + juice of 1

PREP: Wash the zucchini and pat dry, then cut off the ends and discard. Use a box grater to coarsely grate the zucchini—don't worry about peeling them first. Put the grated zucchini into a colander in the sink and sprinkle with the salt. Remove the dark green ends of the leeks and discard. Chop the leeks in half lengthwise through the root, then wipe any dirt inside the leeks away with a damp paper towel. Slice finely into crescents. Peel the shallots, cut them in half lengthwise through the root and slice them finely, too. Put the grated zucchini into a clean dish towel; wrap the zucchini tightly and squeeze as much of the liquid from the zucchini as you can.

COOK: Add the oil to a large skillet over medium heat. Add the zucchini, leeks, shallots and lemon zest to the pan. Cook, stirring occasionally, until the vegetables begin to reduce and take on a jam-like consistency, about 15 minutes. Squeeze the lemon juice into the zucchini mixture and cook for a few more minutes, until the liquid in the pan is cooked off.

FINISHING SALTS
FOUR WAYS

Fancy finishing salts are all the rage these days, since they can add a fantastic punch of flavor to a dish. But you don't need to break the bank buying them—it's really simple to make your own! Here are some flavor combinations for you to start with—when you make your own flavors, remember that you either need to use dried herbs and citrus zest or dry them in the oven yourself once mixed with the salt. Both methods are included here.

EACH MAKES ¼ CUP (60 G)

GRAPEFRUIT-LIME SALT

¼ cup (60 g) coarse or flaky kosher salt

2 tsp (6 g) fresh organic, unwaxed grapefruit zest

1 tsp (2 g) fresh organic, unwaxed lime zest

DRY: Preheat the oven to 200°F (95°C). Mix together the salt and zest. Line a baking tray with parchment paper and spread the salt mixture out on it in an even layer. Bake until the zest is dry and crumbles when squeezed between your fingers about 30 minutes. Once the salt has cooled, mix it with your hands to break up the crystals that have stuck together. Transfer to an airtight container.

USE: This is great with roast chicken and white fish, or sprinkled over fresh fruit salads. Try it with the Braised Spring Chicken (page 79).

LAVENDER-MARJORAM SALT

1 tbsp (1 g) dried lavender buds, divided

1 tsp (1 g) dried marjoram

¼ cup (60 g) coarse or flaky kosher salt

BLEND: Reserve 1 teaspoon of the lavender. Add the remaining lavender and marjoram to a spice grinder and pulse until combined into a coarse powder—don't overprocess, or you will end up with lavender dust! Mix the ground lavender and marjoram with the salt and reserved buds. Transfer to an airtight container. You can substitute oregano for the marjoram, if you wish.

USE: This is wonderful with mushrooms or lamb dishes. It also goes well with carob, try it with the Spiced Banana-Carob Pudding (page 187).

ROSEMARY-LEEK SALT

2 tsp (1 g) dried leek

1 tsp (1 g) dried rosemary

¼ cup (60 g) coarse or flaky kosher salt

BLEND: Add the leek and rosemary to a spice grinder and pulse until combined into a coarse powder—don't over process, or you will end up with herb dust! Mix the ground leek and rosemary with the salt and transfer to an airtight container. You can substitute 1 teaspoon onion powder for the leek, if you wish.

USE: Pair this salt with roast beef or roast vegetables. Try it with the Sweet Potato & Parsnip Mash (page 111).

UMAMI SALT

2 tsp (3 g) dried shrimp

1 tsp (3 g) kelp flakes

¼ cup (60 g) coarse or flaky salt

BLEND: Add all the dried shrimp to a spice grinder and pulse until combined into a coarse powder—don't over-process, or you will end up with shrimp dust! Mix the ground shrimp with the kelp flakes and salt. Transfer to an airtight container.

USE: Sprinkle over Asian-inspired foods. Try it with the Hot and Sour Soup (page 114).

HORSERADISH
TWO WAYS

Horseradish adds a fiery burst of flavor and is one of the only AIP-friendly ways to get any kind of "heat" into your food. The cool thing about that heat is that it comes from the mustard oil that is generated when fresh horseradish root is cut—and that oil has antibacterial properties in addition to its pungent odor!

SIMPLE HORSERADISH

MAKES ABOUT 10 OZ (285 G)

8 oz (225 g) fresh horseradish root
¾ cup (180 ml) white wine vinegar
1 tsp (5 g) salt

GRATE: Wearing gloves, peel the horseradish root, making sure not to leave behind any of the tough, woody outer layer. Use the coarse grating blade on your food processor to grate the horseradish root. Remove the grating blade and replace it with the S-blade. Add the salt and vinegar to the bowl, then pulse until the horseradish and vinegar are combined. If you like your horseradish smooth, you can process the mixture longer until it is at the consistency you prefer. Transfer to a mason jar and refrigerate until needed.

HORSERADISH SAUCE

MAKES 1 CUP (240 ML)

1 cup (240 ml) Eggless "Mayo" (page 196)
¼ cup (60 ml) Simple Horseradish, above

BLEND: Using an immersion blender or mini food processor, combine the "mayo" and horseradish, processing until completely smooth.

TACO SEASONING

You don't need to reach for an MSG-filled seasoning packet to make non-inflammatory taco meat! You can use this as a base for Slow Cooker Bison "Chili" (page 43) and Steak Fajitas (page 64), too!

MAKES ½ CUP (60 G)

¼ cup (12 g) dried oregano leaves
2 tbsp (6 g) dried thyme
2 tbsp (20 g) garlic powder
2 tsp (8 g) onion powder
2 tsp (2 g) ground cinnamon
2 tsp (4 g) ground ginger
2 tsp (1 g) dried fenugreek leaves
1 tsp (1 g) ground dried lime (see note)
1 tsp (1 g) ground mace
½ tsp ground turmeric

GRIND: Add all ingredients to a spice grinder or coffee mill and pulse until you have a fine powder.

NOTE: You can find dried ground lime at Middle Eastern or international stores and markets. It adds a slightly sour and almost smoky flavor that replaces the citrusy notes of coriander seed and really makes this seasoning mix shine.

JICAMA "RAITA"
WITH MINT

Traditionally, raita is a yogurt-based sauce, dip or condiment that is often served with curries and is usually combined with cucumber for a refreshing and cooling taste. Here I've replaced the yogurt with coconut cream and some lime juice to mimic the tanginess of yogurt and to make the recipe AIP friendly—but I've also swapped in jicama for the cucumber. The jicama gives a deliciously satisfying crunch that makes a tasty contrast to the smooth coconut cream. Make sure that you use fresh jicama here—older jicama can become bitter, which is not what we want!

SERVES 6-8

1⅓ cups (320 ml) coconut cream

¼ cup (10 g) fresh mint leaves, minced

2 tbsp (30 ml) lime juice

½ clove garlic, peeled and minced finely

⅛ tsp salt

1½ cups (180 g) coarsely grated, peeled jicama

MIX: In a bowl, whisk the coconut cream until smooth. Add all remaining ingredients except the jicama and stir to combine. Stir through the jicama until the "raita" is evenly combined.

CHILL: Cover the bowl and refrigerate until chilled, about 30 minutes, before serving. Serve as a dip or with salads. If used as a condiment on the side of hot dishes, keep the "raita" separate as additional heat will melt the coconut cream. If making ahead, refrigerate and let the "raita" sit at room temperature for about 30 minutes before serving. Stir before serving.

PITA WEDGES

If you're looking for the perfect way to eat dip, it's slathered on top of these addictively crispy-chewy pita wedges! Lightly seasoned with oregano, these wedges are great for dipping and have a nice almost-grilled flavor from the browning that happens when they're cooked on a hot baking tray.

SERVES 2

¾ cup (90 g) tapioca flour

1½ tbsp. (15 g) coconut flour

½ tsp salt

½ tsp dried oregano leaves

¼ cup (60 ml) coconut milk

2 tbsp (30 ml) water

1½ tbsp (22 ml) melted coconut oil

1 tbsp (15 ml) honey

MIX: Preheat the oven to 450°F (230°C) and put a baking tray into the oven. Mix together all the dry ingredients in a bowl. Use an immersion blender to mix together the liquid ingredients. Make a well in the center of the dry ingredients and pour in the liquids. Use a spatula to cut the liquids into the dry ingredients until you have a uniform, soft dough.

BAKE: Cut a piece of parchment paper to fit your baking tray. Divide the dough into two equal-size pieces and press each one out gently into a 6-inch (15-cm) circle with your hands on the parchment paper. Remove the hot baking tray from the oven and place the parchment paper and dough on the tray carefully. Bake the pita rounds for 10-12 minutes, until the dough is fully cooked and lightly browned on the bottom and edges. Transfer the pita to a wire rack to cool enough to handle. Cut each round into 8 even-size wedges. These are best eaten as soon as they are made, since they become chewier over time.

CRUNCHY SALAD OR SUNDAE TOPPERS

One of the things that is sometimes missing on the AIP is the satisfaction of eating something crunchy. Not "raw carrot" crunchy, more like "salty snack" crunchy. You can bring a little crunch back if you make these plantain or banana chip snacks—if you crush them like in the recipes below, you can even use them to top salads with the savory version or desserts with the sweet variety. You're welcome!

MAKES 2 CUPS (420 G)

CRUNCHY SALAD TOPPER

2 green plantains

3 tbsp (45 ml) coconut or avocado oil

2 tsp (8 g) garlic powder

½ tsp salt

CRISP: Preheat the oven to 350°F (175°C). Line a baking tray with parchment paper. Cut the ends from the plantains, then cut each in half. Score the skin along the ridges and carefully peel away and discard the skin. Use a mandoline to slice the plantain into ⅛ inch (3 mm) thick chips. Toss the sliced plantain with the oil, garlic powder and salt. Lay the plantain chips on the lined baking tray. Bake for 20-25 minutes, until just starting to crisp, but don't let the chips brown. Spread out onto some paper towels to cool.

CRUSH: Add the cooled plantain chips to the bowl of a food processor and pulse until they are a good size to sprinkle over salads. Store in an airtight container.

CRUNCHY SUNDAE TOPPER

2 cups (160 g) unsweetened banana chips

2 tbsp (30 ml) coconut or avocado oil

1 tbsp (3 g) ground cinnamon

1 tbsp (15 ml) honey (optional)

Follow the same method as used above for the Crunchy Salad Topper, substituting 2 cups (160 g) of unsweetened banana chips for the plantain chips. Toss them with 2 tablespoons (30 ml) of coconut or avocado oil, with 1 tablespoon (3 g) ground cinnamon instead of the garlic powder and omitting the salt. If you like, you can also add 1 tablespoon (15 ml) of honey before baking. Use the same method as for the Crunchy Salad Topper, but cook 5-8 minutes.

TIP: Check to ensure that the banana chips are cooked in an acceptable AIP-friendly oil, like coconut oil.

THE BEST BROTHS

The commercially made broths you can find in stores can't hold a candle to the real thing: slow simmered batches of bones with fresh vegetables produce a broth that is full of the natural gelatin that makes broth so nourishing and gut healing. The best part? You'll not only be making nutritious homemade broths, but saving money, too! Soup bones are inexpensive and—even better—you can make broths using your own saved bones. I like to keep a few bags in the freezer to store soup bones by type of protein—when the bags are full, I make new batches of broth. The longer the broth is simmered, the more the bones will break down, which means the higher the content of minerals like calcium and magnesium will be. I like to start each day with a mug of seasoned bone broth to get its amazing health benefits first thing. You can also use these broths to make soups and sauces, or add flavor to simple sautéed vegetables.

BEEF BROTH

The secret weapon in this broth is the neck bones. They add a richer meaty flavor and a boost of collagen that makes this my favorite beef broth. To get a deeper, richer color, I add onion skins, but you can leave them out if you don't mind having a lighter-colored beef broth. I don't personally like to add salt or herbs to my broth while it's simmering because that way I can use it for a range of different dishes, but you can add those to taste if you wish, especially if you are making the broth specifically to drink on its own.

MAKES 4 QUARTS (3.7 L)

3 lbs (1.4 kg) beef soup bones

2 lbs (900 g) beef neck bones

1 onion

2 carrots

2 leeks

2 sticks celery

3 tbsp (45 ml) apple cider vinegar

Enough water to cover the bones

4 extra onion skins (optional, for color)

ROAST: Preheat the oven to 400°F (205°C). Line a baking tray or two—depending on the size and cut of your bones, you may need two. Lay the bones out on the baking tray(s) and roast for 1 hour.

SIMMER: Transfer the roasted bones to the bottom of a large stock pot. Roughly chop the onion, carrots, leeks and celery. I like to add extra onion skins for color, usually from about 4 onions. I save them in the freezer as I use onions for other recipes. Pour in the apple cider vinegar and enough water to cover the bones—if you want to add salt or herbs, pop them in now. Bring the water to a simmer and keep the pot simmering, covered, for 8–48 hours, topping the water off whenever it gets low. Remove and discard the bones and vegetable scraps. Strain the broth through a fine-mesh sieve to get rid of any sediment, then carefully pour the broth into jars or containers. This broth is so rich, it will gel almost solid in the refrigerator—that is normal and a great sign that it is filled with gut-healing collagen.

CHICKEN OR PORK BROTH

You can't go wrong with chicken broth. I like to make pork broth, too, so I don't waste any bones in my kitchen! You can use it interchangeably with chicken broth in most recipes. The chicken feet sound bizarre, I know, but they are a great source of extra nutrition because of the collagen in them. You can buy them ready-peeled in whole food stores.

MAKES 4 QUARTS (3.7 L)

4 lbs (1.4 kg) chicken or pork bones
1 lb (454 g) peeled chicken feet
1 onion
2 carrots
2 leeks
2 sticks celery
3 tbsp (45 ml) apple cider vinegar
Enough water to cover the bones

SIMMER: Add the chicken bones and feet to a large stock pot. Roughly chop the onion, carrots, leek and celery. Pour in the apple cider vinegar and enough water to cover the bones—if you want to add salt or herbs, pop them in now. Bring the water to a boil and skim off any foam from the top. Lower the heat to a simmer and keep the pot simmering, covered, for 8–48 hours, topping the water off whenever it gets low. Remove and discard the bones and vegetable scraps. Strain the broth through a fine mesh sieve to get rid of any sediment, then carefully pour the broth into jars or containers. This broth is so rich, it will gel almost solid in the refrigerator—that is normal and a great sign that it is filled with gut-healing collagen.

SEAFOOD STOCK

This broth doesn't need to simmer anywhere near as long as bone broths and can be made with scraps. I save shrimp shells and keep any fish bones in the freezer until I have enough to make this stock.

MAKES 2 QUARTS (1.9 L)

2 lbs (900 g) shrimp shells or fish bones
Enough water to cover the shells

SIMMER: Add the shrimp shells and/or the fish bones to a saucepan. Bring the water to a boil and skim off any foam from the top. Lower the heat to a simmer and keep the pot simmering for about 1 hour. Remove and discard the shells or bones. Strain the broth through a fine-mesh sieve to get rid of any sediment, then carefully pour the broth into jars or containers.

7

MAKE
A MENU

The recipes in this book can be combined in lots of different ways to put together meals however you like. To give you a little inspiration, I've put together a few themed sample menus so you can see how everything can come together. You might be on the AIP, but you can still have Taco Tuesday or Fajita Friday!

When using these menus, I've shown you which recipes or components can be made ahead of time and those that need to be made fresh at meal time. The instructions that are in bold refer to specific steps within the original recipes so that you know exactly which parts of the recipe you're following as you go.

INDIAN FEAST

SERVES 6+

CHICKEN PUMPKIN CURRY (PAGE 83)
INDIAN SPICED LEMON "RICE" (PAGE 163)
JICAMA RAITA (PAGE 221)
ROASTED OKRA WITH HOT & SOUR DIPPING SAUCE (PAGE 155)

MAKE AHEAD:

- **MARINATE** the chicken, chill until needed, up to overnight.

- Start to make the "rice," following the **BAKE** step, then refrigerate once cooked.

- **MIX** and **CHILL** the Jicama Raita.

- Make the Hot & Sour Dipping Sauce to go with the Roasted Okra, omitting the fresh cilantro from the **MIX** step. Cover and chill.

MAKE AT MEAL TIME:

- Take the Jicama Raita & Hot & Sour Dipping Sauce out of the fridge and let come to room temperature.

- Finish the Chicken Pumpkin Curry and keep it warm at a low **SIMMER**.

- While the curry is simmering, **ROAST** the okra. **SEASON** and warm the "rice" on the stovetop.

- Add the cilantro to the Hot & Sour Dipping Sauce before serving.

THAI TAKEOUT

SERSS 6+

SERVES 6+

GRILLED THAI BEEF SKEWERS (PAGE 49)
THAI CHICKEN SOUP (PAGE 48)
GREEN PAPAYA SALAD WITH SHRIMP & RADISHES (PAGE 139)

MAKE AHEAD:

- **MARINATE** the beef for the skewers. Refrigerate until needed, up to overnight.

- Follow the **COOK** and **SIMMER** instructions for the Thai Chicken Soup, then chill until needed.

- Make the Green Papaya Salad dressing, then refrigerate the shredded papaya and dressing separately.

MAKE AT MEAL TIME:

- **ASSEMBLE** the beef skewers, threading the beef with pineapple and green onions.

- **BLANCH** the shrimp for the Green Papaya Salad and toss with the shredded papaya, then return to the refrigerator while you cook the beef.

- **GRILL** or broil the Thai Beef Skewers.

- Dress the Green Papaya Salad and **TOSS** with the green onions, herbs and radishes before serving.

- Gently reheat the Thai Chicken Soup, then add the spinach to **WILT** and garnish with green onions and herbs before serving.

BBQ & FIXIN'S

SERVES 6+

2-3 RACKS OF PERFECT OVEN BAKED BBQ RIBS (PAGE 54)
GERMAN POTATO SALAD (PAGE 158)
PURPLE SLAW WITH FENNEL AND DILL (PAGE 179)
CIDER-BRAISED GREENS (PAGE 168)

MAKE AHEAD:

- Make, cook and cool the BBQ Sauce for the ribs. Keep in the fridge until needed.

- Make the German Potato Salad and chill until needed.

- Make and dress the Purple Slaw and chill until needed.

MAKE AT MEAL TIME:

- **PREP** and **COOK** the Oven Baked Ribs.

- While the ribs are baking, and with about 30 minutes until they need to be broiled, cook the Cider-Braised Greens and keep warm.

- Remove the German Potato Salad from the fridge and toss with a little extra olive oil and vinegar just before serving.

- Baste and **BROIL** the ribs.

GET YOUR GREEK ON

SERVES 6+

SUMMER SQUASH SOUP WITH LEMON (PAGE 161)

GREEK "COUSCOUS" SALAD (PAGE 173)

LAMB LETTUCE CUPS WITH CUCUMBER SAUCE (PAGE 84)

PITA WEDGES (PAGE 222)

MAKE AHEAD:

- Make the Summer Squash Soup, **BLEND** and refrigerate it until needed.

- **ROAST** the cauliflower and make the dressing for the "couscous" salad. Refrigerate them separately.

- Make, **BLEND** and chill the Cucumber Sauce to go with the Lamb Lettuce Cups.

MAKE AT MEAL TIME:

- Chop the remaining "couscous" ingredients and **TOSS** the salad to combine with the dressing.

- **BLEND**, **MIX** and roll out the dough for the Pita Wedges.

- Start cooking the filling for the Lamb Lettuce Cups—preheat the oven for the Pita Wedges once the lamb is in the pan browning.

- Keep the lamb filling warm while you **BAKE** the Pita Wedges.

- While the Pita Wedges are cooling on a wire rack, gently reheat the Summer Squash Soup if serving it warm. If not, keep it chilled until ready to serve.

FAJITA NIGHT

SERVES 4

STEAK FAJITAS (PAGE 64)
NO-NIGHTSHADE SALSA (PAGE 205)
GRILLED PINEAPPLE GUACAMOLE (PAGE 213)

MAKE AHEAD:

- **MARINATE** the steak in the refrigerator.

- **BLEND** together the No-Nightshade Salsa and chill until needed.

MAKE AT MEAL TIME:

- Make the Grilled Pineapple Guacamole. Cover and chill while you cook the steak and vegetables.

- **SEAR** the steak and rest it while you prep the vegetables.

- **GRILL** the fajita vegetables, then slice the steaks across the grain. Pile the fajita meat and vegetables on a serving platter.

GO, TEAM!

SERVES 8+

GLAZED & BAKED CHICKEN WINGS (PAGE 63)
BBQ SAUCE (PAGE 201)
PARSNIP WEDGES WITH GARLIC "MAYO" DIPPING SAUCE (PAGE 136)
SPINACH ARTICHOKE DIP (PAGE 209)

MAKE AHEAD:

- **MARINATE** the Glazed & Baked Chicken Wings, up to overnight.

- Make the BBQ Sauce and refrigerate until needed.

- **BLEND** together the Garlic "Mayo" Dipping Sauce and chill.

- Make the Spinach Artichoke Dip and refrigerate it until needed.

MAKE AT MEAL TIME:

- Take out the Garlic "Mayo" Dipping Sauce to allow it to soften.

- **BAKE** the Chicken Wings.

- While the Chicken Wings are baking, prep and **BOIL** the Parsnip Wedges.

- **ROAST** the Parsnip Wedges.

- While the Parsnip Wedges are roasting, warm through the Spinach Artichoke Dip.

- Serve the Chicken Wings with the BBQ Sauce on the side.

PICNIC OR PATIO LUNCH

SERVES 4+

WATERMELON GAZPACHO (PAGE 152)
THE ULTIMATE LIVER-HATER'S PÂTÉ (PAGE 68)
WARM CHICKEN "GRAIN" SALAD (PAGE 44)

MAKE AHEAD:

- Make and chill the Watermelon Gazpacho.

- **COOK** and **CHILL** the Ultimate Liver-Hater's Pâté.

- **ROAST** the vegetables for the Warm Chicken "Grain" Salad.

- Cut and prep the vegetables to serve with the Ultimate Liver-Hater's Pâté and chill until needed.

MAKE AT MEAL TIME:

- **COOK** the chicken for the "Grain" Salad and toss all ingredients together.

SWEDISH MEATBALL PLATE

SERVES 4

CHERRY SAUCE WITH THYME (PAGE 214)
BAKED SWEDISH MEATBALLS (PAGE 36)
WHIPPED SWEET POTATOES (PAGE 180)

MAKE AHEAD:

- Make the Cherry Sauce With Thyme and refrigerate until needed.

- Make and roll the Baked Swedish Meatballs, then chill until needed.

MAKE AT MEAL TIME:

- **BAKE** the Swedish Meatballs and rest them.

- While the Swedish Meatballs are baking, **SIMMER** the sweet potatoes. Make sure to use white sweet potatoes here, if you can, since they are less sweet.

- **REDUCE** the gravy for the Swedish Meatballs and add them to the pan to warm through.

- **WHIP** the Sweet Potatoes.

- Serve the Swedish Meatballs and Whipped Sweet Potatoes with the Cherry Sauce on the side.

ACKNOWLEDGMENTS

I couldn't have written this book without my husband: partner in crime, chief taste tester, now-expert-grocery-store-navigator and patient eater of all the cold meals that happen when you live with somebody who is testing and photographing recipes all day, every day. I guess I owe you a few hot meals...

None of this would have happened in the first place if it wasn't for my friend and nest-pusher, Steph, who inspires me every day to be better and more badass than the day before. I owe you more thanks than you know!

Amy and Ciarra—you kept me sane, made me laugh and helped me through a few not-so-perfect situations like Plumbergate 2014. Ladies, I'll be showing my appreciation in the form of pork belly, I promise!

Peter, I owe you a favor in return for your meatball expertise! And fluency in Swedish, because goodness knows what would have happened if I'd tried to translate Swedish on my own...

I also want to thank the team at Page Street Publishing who have given me the opportunity to do what I love and turn my vision for this book into a reality with all their help, support and encouragement. We just won't mention the coffee explosion again, okay?

Last but not least, I'd like to thank Dr. Sarah Ballantyne, PhD, for her tireless research and work in creating, explaining and spreading the word about the AIP. Without her, I would probably not have ever come across the AIP, this book would never have happened and I would not be on my path to healing.

ABOUT THE AUTHOR

RACHAEL BRYANT is the blogger behind the scenes of meatified.com, which she started as a way to keep her recipes in one place when she first began eating Paleo. The name was a little bit of a joke: as a former vegetarian, switching to Paleo was quite a dietary U-turn. It's a little pun on how she had expected that she would be eating more meat than vegetables. In reality, she probably eats more vegetables now than she ever did as a vegetarian!

Rachael turned to the Paleo diet originally to help manage the symptoms of Hashimoto's disease. After experiencing a huge improvement in her symptoms on the Paleo diet, she came across the AIP and realized that it was the missing piece of her personal healing puzzle!

Realizing how amazing she felt while eating nourishing food with simple ingredients, and how much she loved the challenge of coming up with new, tasty recipes, her mission now is to show others how to bring real food and healing into their own lives, without going crazy or breaking the bank in the process.

INDEX